The topic of i~~dentity~~ is ~~perhaps~~ one of the most popular in our day. We are fascinated by what it promises, which is why so many undertake the journey to understand it. At its best, the study of identity enriches our self-knowledge, but far too often the path to identity falls into a rut, stuck in the trench of self-preoccupation. Christy Rood is well aware of this peril, and offers herself as a wise and winsome guide. With the help of research, cultural analysis, and theological grounding, she avoids the pitfalls that others have fallen into, instead offering a smart, inspiring, and Christ-centered path to understanding the gift of identity.

Sharon Hodde Miller, Author of *Nice: Why We Love to Be Liked and How God Calls Us to More*

Grounded in rich theology and psychology, *Tracing the Thread* invites us to reframe our identity by diving into the narratives we've lived by. Christy guides us away from the crippling effect of sin management and into the deeper stories that shape our beliefs and behavior. Serving as both friend and teacher, she shows us how to rewrite a more truthful story that honors the way God designed us. At once sobering and freeing, read this book when you're ready to change.

Beth Bruno, Author of *A Voice Becoming* and host of the *Fierce and Lovely* podcast

Have you ever struggled with your identity? Who are you? Why are you here? I believe all of us have at some level or another. *Tracing the Thread* is an insightful and compelling companion to these deeply personal examining questions. Not only does Christy Rood explore factors in identity formation like parental love, tribes you belong to, and the voice you listen to—more importantly, she centers the whole discussion on the gospel of Jesus Christ. Only God can answer your deepest questions of identity. Our identity in Christ is formed not by what we do, but by what Christ has done. There is a lot of wisdom in this book.

Matt Capps, Senior Pastor, Fairview Baptist Church, Apex, NC

The world is full of books about discipleship. And yet, if we're honest, the great scandal of the church today is the lack of transformation. It is not uncommon for someone to be an active part of a church, holding leadership positions, teaching bible studies, and yet, over the years being more or less the same person they've always been. We're not that much different from those outside the church. Christy Rood has given a great gift to the church in her very practical and detailed book, *Tracing the Thread: Examining the Story of Self for Lasting Change.* Christy skillfully explores why it is so difficult to change. We have ingrained habits of the mind and body that keep us stuck in narratives that were often firmly established in early childhood. Why do afflictive emotions such as anger, fear, shame, anxiety, insecurity, inadequacy, etc. continue to dominate our internal world and threaten our relationships? Christy, demonstrating that she is honestly and courageously walking this road of transformation herself, invites us to look into the details of our inner world and invite the power of the Holy Spirit to bring actual change. Not white-knuckled, effort-in-the-moment change, but real, authentic, changing-the-person-I-actually am change. As Dallas Willard would say, where I am routinely and easily learning how to live my life as Jesus would if he were I. This is the true narrow way. The way of losing our life in order to find it. Christy is a winsome and most excellent guide into the details of authentic transformation. Read this book with others and engage in courageous and honest conversations of how we came to be who we currently are, and what it would take to be substantially changed from the inside out.

Kent Carlson, Vice President of Leadership Formation, North American Baptists, Inc.

As a pastor of 30 years who is venturing into the field of mental health, I read *Tracing the Thread* while seeking answers to a dilemma I am facing. During a discussion in group therapy at a psychiatric hospital a person who is a committed Christian and values their faith admitted that going back to church feels so lonely after her experience in group therapy. I might excuse this as the feeling of one person if it were not for the nodding heads of agreement in that room. After reading Christy's book I wonder how different church would feel if people believed their true identity? How inviting would church become for broken people who need a safe place to share and discover who they truly are in Jesus's eyes?

John Barnett, Senior Pastor, Community Bible Church, Easley, SC

Tracing the Thread

TRACING
THE
THREAD

Examining the Story of Self
for Lasting Change

Christy Rood

foreword by **Hannah Anderson**

Gospel-Centered Discipleship

Tracing the Thread:
Examining the Story of Self for Lasting Change

© 2020 Christy Rood
All rights reserved.

GCD Books
Austin, TX

GCD Books is a ministry of Gospel-Centered Discipleship. Our purpose is to produce resources that make, mature, and multiply disciples of Jesus.

To get more resources from Gospel-Centered Discipleship, visit us at GCDiscipleship.com/Books and follow us on Twitter @GCDiscipleship.

Front cover design: Laura Schembre of Copper Street Design (copper-streetdesign.com)
Back cover & interior design: Benjamin Vrbicek (benjaminvrbicek.com)

ISBN 13: 978-0-578-65609-0
ISBN 10: 0-578-65609-4

For my earthly father,
whose love I have never doubted.
You made it easy for me to believe
I am loved by my heavenly one.

CONTENTS

BY HANNAH ANDERSON

Sometime in the winter of 2014, a large brown shipping box landed at my kitchen door. It weighed, easily, fifty pounds, and as I dragged it inside and hefted it onto my kitchen table, my heart raced and my breath came short and quick--and not just from the sudden physical exertion. I knew what was inside. Grabbing a pair of scissors, I sliced open the flaps, and shoved aside the brown paper that a warehouse worker had stuffed into the box to protect its contents. And there it was. My first book. Or more, accurately fifty copies of my first book.

As first books go, mine was not remarkable. But for me, *Made for More* was more than a foray into publishing. It was the outworking of a more private conversation that I'd been having with friends (and myself) for several years. It was a conversation about who I was and where I belonged in the world. It was, much like the book you're holding in your hands, a book about identity.

We really shouldn't be surprised when authors begin their catalogs writing on identity. What we believe about ourselves, our purpose and place in this world, and to whom we belong is the foundation of everything else that we think or do. It's almost as if we have to get this one thing right before anything else can make sense. So while we shouldn't be surprised when a first time author tackles such existential questions, we *should* be surprised when a first time author can write with clarity, precision, and intent on these questions. We *should* be surprised when a first time author can explore the topic of identity and actually add to the conversation. We *should* be surprised when a first time author can offer, not only her unique perspective, but practical advice and spiritual guidance for your own journey to know yourself.

Which is exactly why I believe this book, *Tracing the Thread,* will surprise—and help—you.

In *Tracing the Thread*, Christy Rood shows us how our identity (and false identities) lies at the root of our unwanted behavior, choices, and habits. Our sense of our ourselves and how we relate to the world explain why we struggle to change, why we interact with people as we do, and why simple mandates to "just do the right thing" are so often ineffective. Showing how false identities develop through childhood, our tribes, and the messages we receive, Rood also shows how finding true identity in the gospel can lead to lasting peace and purpose.

If you've read *my* first book, you'll know that it is undeniably "big picture." I can't help but fly at thirty-thousand feet especially when it comes to questions of human identity and purpose. But as beautiful a vista as this may offer, it's not very helpful in sorting out the messy details of life. After all, if we cannot name the ways in which our false identities triumph over our true identity, we'll never be able to live the grand beautiful live that we long for.

And this is the benefit of *Tracing the Thread.* Starting with that "big picture" of identity as God's image bearers, Rood quickly zooms in on the details, showing how why and how we've developed other identities. Then, using personal story, philosophy, Scripture, and relevant psychology, she charts a clear and accurate path from where we are to where we all hope to be. Connecting the dots this way, she leads us beyond "big picture" to practical application, offering hope that the abundant life we long for is not so far out of our reach as it might initially seem.

I don't know what went through Rood's head when a big brown shipping box landed on her doorstep recently. I'm sure, like me, she experienced a mixture of excitement, vulnerability, and disbelief. I also hope she experienced a bit of joy, the kind of joy that comes from knowing that your private questions and personal struggles have meaning beyond themselves. The kind of joy that comes from knowing who you are and where you belong in this world.

The kind of joy that comes from knowing that your journey has paved the way for others.

Hannah Anderson

PARADIGM SHIFTS

A t least once a week, I am an emotional wreck. One minute I am calm and mostly sane and within the next my eyes are watering, and I'm in need of a good hug.

If you're a parent of older kids and are on Facebook, you know how quickly your mood can shift when Facebook shows you a flashback memory from three, five, or ten years ago. It wrecks you, doesn't it? You settle on the couch with your morning coffee and open up Facebook to see what your friends are up to and *BAM*. You get sucker punched by the sweet, smiling, younger face of one of your kids. In a flash, you are transported back to the day the photo was taken. You hear their cute little voices and feel their tiny hands in yours. You laugh at their silly antics and remember a simpler time when your worries revolved around keeping them clean, fed, and entertained. The passing of time is mysterious. You don't notice the changes in your kids from day to day or even month to month. You are too busy going to the next soccer game, dance recital, band concert, or science fair. But when a photo or video picks you up and plops you back in time, it can be shocking to see how drastically your kids' faces and bodies have changed.

Most of my paradigm shifts have occurred slowly and without perception, just like the unnoticed growth of my children. Similar to the shock I experience when looking upon an old, cherished memory, the only way I can see how radically my perspectives have changed is to go back and read a book, listen to a speaker, or chat with a friend who thinks the way I used to think. It is jarring. This is how my paradigm regarding how Christians grow and change has similarly shifted and developed. I can't point to a single "Aha" moment, a specific sermon or book, or even a defining experience that triggered the shift, but when I reenter the thought world of my religious past, I am often surprised by how far I have come.

The Formula for Change

Many of us can immediately call to mind an area in our lives where, despite our best efforts, we just couldn't seem to turn the corner toward real and lasting change. Perhaps, like me, you are a chronic people-pleaser, or maybe you keep loading up your schedule to bolster your feeling of significance. Maybe you flare up quickly in anger, especially toward those you love most, or you find yourself unable to quit habits that provide you comfort or dull your anxiety. Perhaps your recurring behaviors have damaged relationships, caused you to withdraw and isolate yourself, or led you to berate or even harm yourself.

When we planted a new church sixteen years ago, I thought I understood how to help someone change. I had been taught that it came down to a basic war between the old and new natures, and that the battles were won by continuously acknowledging and confessing sin, repenting, asking for forgiveness, and putting new habits into place to prevent a return to sinful behavior. Ephesians 4 was the template for this formula for change; simply "Put off your old self . . . [and] put on the new self." Like a wardrobe update, it sounded fairly straightforward. If you want to change, simply stop sinning and start living rightly.

A few years into the trenches of attempting to pastor broken people as a broken person myself, I began to realize this formula for change was too simplistic for the average individual. In fact, not only was it ineffective to tell people to "just stop sinning," but in some cases, it also created a new crop of problems. The more they tried to change and failed, the worse they felt about themselves and the higher the probability they would eventually quit trying altogether.

How We Talk about the Problem

It wasn't just the formula for change, however, that I found to be limited in effectiveness. Rather it was how we talked about the problem. I used to think I would be giving people excuses for their bad behavior if I failed to name it sin, and if I did not call them to confess and repent. If I blamed a woman's anger on mental illness, for example, when she lashed out at her husband during a bipolar episode, I would be removing her choice from the equation and thus making it harder for her to change. We previously spoke about all behavior as good or bad, right or wrong, without exploring any causation beyond the sin nature. In this way of teaching, many root causes were ignored, and guilt and shame draped in heavy layers on the shoulders of many Christians. I'm embarrassed now by my simplistic, harmful advice to struggling parishioners. If any of you are reading, I am sorry, and I pray the damage was minimal.

In our early years of ministry, we also over-emphasized human depravity. Almost every sermon could be boiled down to "We are broken and depraved. We need grace. Thank you, Jesus for taking on our sin and shame and showing us mercy on the cross." These are absolutely true statements, but a steady, exclusive diet of this teaching can tend to make us see God as perpetually disappointed with us, dutifully and robotically offering us forgiveness out of sheer adherence to his nature. We can forget that while humans are broken and depraved, we are also prized by our Creator, created for glory, and in need of a return to our created ideal. It took me a long time to realize that trusting in God's great love for his children is a much more powerful foundation for change than fearing his disappointment and displeasure.

A few years into ministry, I realized I needed a deeper, more effective, longer-lasting, foundational answer to my questions of how to help people change, as well as new language to talk about the problem. I needed it for myself, and I needed it for others.

Identity As the Key

I'm not sure when my paradigm shifted, but through experiences of walking with people in trials, trying to change my own attitudes and actions, and reading and studying, I began to understand over time that speaking about sin as an isolated event without delving into the motives and beliefs that drive these sinful actions was a mistake. I began to believe that changing foundational identity was a more effective method of change. I came to see that the answer had more to do with *being* than *doing.* If we could help people *believe* differently about themselves, they would begin to *behave* differently.

When my husband and I walked with people through chronic infidelity, for example, rather than piling on shame by emphasizing how their sin displeased God and then giving them a list of behaviors to change, we first began to dig into their core identity beliefs. More often than not, they believed they were inherently worthless, and that lie was driving their behavior. The only way that person could see true and lasting change was to change their belief about themselves from worthless to highly valued and fully loved.

But are these kinds of radical shifts even possible? Can we change how we see ourselves?

Going Back to Go Forward

In his book *Emotionally Healthy Spirituality*, Peter Scazzero points out what I believe is the often-neglected step in the Christian's path toward change. Scazzero writes, "The work of growing in Christ (what theologians call sanctification) does not mean we don't go back to the past as we press ahead to what God has for us. It actually demands we go back in order to break free from unhealthy patterns that prevent us from loving ourselves and others as God designed."[1]

---

[1] Peter Scazzero, *Emotionally Healthy Spirituality* (Grand Rapids: Zondervan, 2014), 28.

Understanding identity in Christ as the key to lasting change was step one for me in my personal life and ministry experience. The second step was figuring out which lies about my identity were driving my harmful behaviors and how they became part of my core beliefs. If I wanted to change and help others change, I would need to trace my story backward to uncover the roots of my damaging identity lies.

As painful as it was, I began to trace every one of my knee-jerk reactions backward by peeling back the layers to the motive underneath, then going deeper still to the lie that fueled the motive. Some of them were fairly obvious, such as my belief that I will only be accepted when I perform well. Other lies could only be discovered during painful seasons of refinement, and I felt them squeezed out of me like the last of the toothpaste.

What I found, though, when I traced the lies back to their origins, was that patterns and categories began to emerge. The vast majority of the lies I believed about myself came from three sources: *the parental love I received, the tribes I belonged to, and the voices I listened to.*

These three cradles of identity, hewn during the earliest years of my life, laid the foundation for my sense of self and greatly impacted the self I chose to be. *The story that was written for me had profound and often unseen effects on the story I was now writing.* If I wanted to change how I wrote my story in the present, I would have to go back to the parts of my story I didn't write—the chapters and paragraphs where my definition of self was penned not by me, but by others, and allow God to overlay them with the truths of who he sees me to be.

Why Another Book on Identity?

In recent years the Christian book market has been inundated with books about identity in Christ. These books have contributed to my paradigm shift and have greatly influenced the writing of this book. Many authors have written extensively about the necessity of seeing ourselves as God's beloved. I am humbly grateful to the many writers who have followed their calling to expound the riches of God's love by assuring us, "You are not what the world makes you. You are children of God."[2]

This book is intended to build on those crucial identity truths and apply them to the earliest years of your life, when your sense of self was taking root. This book is meant to help you understand why you continually put your identity in other things and help you determine how you can break free from these habits. Instead of starting in the middle of the story, where most identity books begin, this book will start at the beginning of your story. Instead of pointing out where you are currently misaligned with your true identity, this book seeks to point out where your misalignments began and guide you in making the corrections at the source in order to change your story going forward.

The first few chapters will address our current culture's obsession with identity and the Christian's response. Then, we will delve into the three cradles of identity. To help you identify the places in your story where your identity was damaged or misinformed, I

---

[2] Henri J.M. Nouwen, *Here and Now: Living in the Spirit* (New York: The Crossroad Publishing Company, 2003), Chapter 9, Kindle Edition.

have included reflection questions at the end of each chapter. If you find it helpful, I encourage you to journal your answers as you read. I've also included several true stories from friends of mine. Perhaps you will see hints of your story in theirs. My hope is that you will find ultimate freedom in re-reading your own story and that you would allow God to help you see yourself the way he sees you.

My prayer is that within the pages of this book you will find not further condemnation but rather hope for healing, restoration, and change.

1

WHAT IS IDENTITY?

There is only one question: Who are you? Every-thing else in life flows from that one question. That is true whether you are a person of faith or not; the identity question is the question.

– Klyne R. Snodgrass[1]

GenMe'ers enjoy unprecedented freedom to pursue what makes them happy and to look past tradi-tional distinctions based on race, gender, and sexual orientation. But their high expectations, combined with an increasingly competitive world, have led to a darker flip side, in which they blame other people for their problems and sink into anxi-ety and depression.

– Jean M Twenge[2]

The word identity has all but run its course in our culture of ever-changing trends. The idea that identity is created and asserted by the individual has seeped unnoticed into the collective consciousness of an entire generation. Most of us

---

[1] Klyne R. Snodgrass, *Who God Says You Are* (Grand Rapids: Wm. B. Eerdmans Publishing Co., 2018), Chapter 1, Kindle Edition.

[2] Jean M. Twenge, *Generation Me – Revised and Updated: Why Today's Young Americans Are More Confident, Assertive, Entitled—and More Miserable Than Ever Before* (New York: Atria Books, 2014), Introduction, Kindle Edition.

can't remember a time when the individual was not the focal point—a time when self-sacrifice was nobler than self-expression; when the community defined the individual and not the other way around; when the question was "How can I contribute?" rather than "How can I be noticed?" It has now faded into the wallpaper of our shared psyche that the gate to a happy life can only be unlocked by figuring out who you are and then asserting and staying true to yourself. We have been raised to believe in the value of the individual above all else, and we have taken this notion to its logical conclusion: tolerance for almost any form of identity expression, no matter how far outside the norm.

Wesley Morris wrote an article in the *New York Times* in October 2015 called "The Year We Obsessed Over Identity." His basic premise is that our country is "in the midst of a great cultural identity migration. Gender roles are merging. Races are being shed . . . we've been made to see how trans- and bi- and poly-ambi-omni we are." Morris attributes this shift not only to the rise of social media and video games, which allow us to create alternative and preferred personas, but also to the rise of reality TV, in particular the hugely popular makeover shows that gave us permission to change ourselves into the people we wish to be. Suddenly, we started asking ourselves, "Do I like who I am?" This led to "Whom do I want to be?" and then to "What is stopping me from becoming that person?" In Morris's words, this quick progression has led to the current "sense of fluidity and permissiveness and a smashing of binaries."[3]

Gender is one of those binaries being smashed. You may have seen the video published online in April 2016 by the Family Policy Institute of Washington where a host interviews college students on the University of Washington campus. The interviewer starts by asking each interviewee what they would think of him if he identified as a woman. All the students say they would be fine with that and, in fact, would applaud him for his bravery in expressing himself in that way. Then he moves to the more absurd by asking, "What if I want to be identified as a Chinese person?" That causes a few of them to pause, faced with the obvious Caucasian face in front of them, but all still reply, "Whatever you want to believe about yourself." From there, his questions become more and more absurd: "What if I said I was a seven-year-old?" and "What if I said I was six-foot-five?" A few students decide there have to be limits to self-expression, but some stick to their guns that people have the right to present themselves as whatever identity they choose.[4]

Race is another identity marker being shed, albeit a little more slowly than gender. In June 2015, a white woman in Spokane was appointed as regional head of the National Association for the Advancement of Colored People (NAACP). Married to a black man, with two biracial children, she claimed she identified

---

[3] Wesley Morris, "The Year We Obsessed Over Identity," *The New York Times Magazine*, October 6, 2015, https://www.nytimes.com/2015/10/11/magazine/the-year-we-obsessed-over-identity.html.

[4] Family Policy Institute of Washington, "Gender Identity: Can a 5'9, White Guy Be a 6'5, Chinese Woman?", April 13, 2016, https://www.youtube.com/user/FPIWASH.

more as a black woman. She even went so far as to darken her skin and perm her hair to make the outside match the inside. Other than some black people who were offended by a white person trying to identify with an oppressed race, many people applauded her for having the courage to break down racial identity barriers by not just accepting people of another race but even by becoming one of them.[5]

Racial and gender distinctions are being rapidly erased by the pervading message that we are all fundamentally the same. This message suggests gender, race, and sexuality are purely social constructs; you can be anything you want to be. Not only is this fluidity tolerated, it is venerated. People who push against old-school societal norms, expressing themselves and their identity in ways that were intolerable even two decades ago, are now hailed as heroes. In fact, the bigger the hurdle, the louder the praise seems to be.

The Fallout

While some good has come out of these cultural shifts, the encouragement to define ourselves however we choose has not turned out how we expected. Instead of weightless freedom at the end of that string, we have found heavy chains. Indeed, we are seeing the wisdom in Kierkegaard's simple statement

[5] Maria L. La Ganga and Matt Pearce, "Rachel Dolezal's Story, a Study of Race and Identity, gets 'Crazier and Crazier,'" *Los Angeles Times*, June 15, 2015, http://www.latimes.com/nation/la-na-spokane-naacp-rachel-dolezal-resigns-20150615-story.html.

"Anxiety is the dizziness of freedom."[6] When the pressure is on the individual to decide who they are and what they can become, there is no one to blame but themselves when they fail to become who they want to be. This anxiety is played out on social media and in the workforce, but it is perhaps most palpable on college campuses. In a study on generational differences in perfectionism, researchers Thomas Curran and Andrew Hill noted a marked increase in social and self-oriented perfectionism in college students in the past thirty years.[7] Another long-term study has concluded that over the past eighty years young Americans are becoming more anxious and depressed. Psychologist and generational researcher Jean Twenge believes this trend has several contributing factors, including an obsession with image, money, and fame, but she also blames isolation and loneliness.[8]

In England, the loneliness epidemic led to the government appointing its first ever "Minister for Loneliness" cabinet member.[9] The decline in face-to-face interactions has definitely made us lonelier, but

---

[6] Soren Kierkegaard, *The Concept of Anxiety: A Simple Psychologically Oriented Deliberation in View of the Dogmatic Problem of Hereditary Sin* (London: Liveright Publishing Corporation, 2014), Introduction, Kindle Edition.

[7] Kristen Lee, "The Unsettling Truth About What's Hurting Today's Students," *Psychology Today*, January 23, 2018, https://www.psychologytoday.com/blog/rethink-your-way-the-good-life/201801/the-unsettling-truth-about-what-s-hurting-today-s.

[8] Jesse Singal, "For 80 Years, Young Americans Have Been Getting More Anxious and Depressed, and No One Is Quite Sure Why," *The Cut*, March 13, 2016, https://www.thecut.com/2016/03/for-80-years-young-americans-have-been-getting-more-anxious-and-depressed.html.

[9] Ceylan Yeginsu, "U.K. Appoints a Minister for Loneliness," The New York Times, January 17, 2018, https://www.nytimes.com/2018/01/17/world/europe/uk-britain-loneliness.html.

how we interact online now versus a decade ago has also contributed. We've shifted from *relating* with one another to *competing* with one another. A recent article about the "mommy internet" details how in the last ten years blogs and Instagram accounts have moved away from sharing the authentic, gritty, relatable side of parenting. Instead these platforms have become a means of advertising carefully-branded, unrealistic perfection. As a result "We've lost a source of support and community, a place to share vulnerability and find like-minded women, and a forum of female expertise and wisdom."[10] This competitive way of relating to one another is a direct result of the modern emphasis on individual identity expression. It has led to men and women feeling alone on their quest for success in a dog-eat-dog world.

The unmooring of individual identity from fixed markers has also contributed to the intense tribalism we see today. From partisan politics to deep racial divides to the #MeToo movement, we have never been more divided into—or more fiercely defensive of—our tribes. *New York Times* columnist David Brooks, quoting philosopher Pascal Bruckner, writes,

> Modern individualism releases each person from social obligation, but "being guided only by the lantern of his own understanding, the individual loses all assurance of a place, an order, a

---

[10] Sarah Pulliam Bailey, "How the Mom Internet Became a Spotless, Sponsored Void," *The Washington Post,* January 26, 2018, https://www.washingtonpost.com/outlook/how-the-mom-internet-became-a-spotless-sponsored-void/2018/01/26/072b46ac-01d6-11e8-bb03-722769454f82_story.html.

definition. He may have gained freedom, but he has lost security."[11]

Tribes, Brooks continues, are the logical places to find security in the dizziness of our newfound freedom. It makes sense to seek safety in groups of people who share our values, especially when we have no anchor but our own fickle selves to sink our identity into.

What is identity from a Christian perspective?

Though identity as a buzzword has run its course, it is more important than ever for Christians to have a firm grasp on both the cultural and biblical definitions. We are warned not to "conform to the pattern of this world, but be transformed by the renewing of [our] mind[s]."[12] In order to not be pulled along by the cultural tide, we must have a clear understanding of not only what culture says but also what God says about this topic. We are called to be agents of change and beacons of light in a broken world.[13] How can we shift the conversation if we are unaware of the truth that will illuminate the darkness? Most importantly, a proper understanding of a Christian's identity has the power to change us in profound ways. There is truth to the secular view that discovering who you are is the secret to a happy life, but the Christian's path to self-discovery diverges drastically from the culture's. And, contrary to secular self-discovery, what

---

[11] David Brooks, "The Retreat to Tribalism," *The New York Times*, January 1, 2018, https://www.nytimes.com/2018/01/01/opinion/the-retreat-to-tribalism.html.

[12] Romans 12:2

[13] Matthew 5:13–14

the Christian finds at the end of that path offers true contentment.

Where did this concept of identity come from? The word identity comes from the sixteenth-century Latin word *identitatem*, which the French turned into *identité*. The root of the word is *idem*, which is translated "sameness." Think *identical*, like a twin, or like the image of your face being reflected back to you in a mirror. The modern understanding of identity, based largely on the psychoanalytical research of Erik Erikson[14] in the 1950s, is the set of beliefs we hold concerning ourselves. These beliefs inform our emotions and motivate our actions.

Where the Christian understanding begins to diverge from the cultural understanding is in the *source* of those beliefs. Timothy Keller is the well-known pastor of Redeemer Presbyterian Church in New York City. In late 2015, he spoke to students at Wheaton College on the subject of identity.[15] He said in times past, or in traditional cultures, the common view was that we *received* our identity from our community—I am my parent's daughter, I am part of this village, etc. Today, the common view is that we *form* our identity through self-exploration and then self-expression. We are told we can determine who we are by looking deep within ourselves, and we are encouraged to then express that identity. Whereas in times past your "self"

---

[14] To read more about Erik Erikson's theory of identity development, here is a chapter from a psychology textbook: https://www   .yumpu.com/en/document/view/7395392/erik-eriksons-theory-of-identity-development.

[15] Tim Keller, "Our Identity: The Christian Alternative to Late Modernity's Story," a sermon given at Wheaton College on November 11, 2015, YouTube video, https://www.youtube.com/watch?v=Ehw87PqTwKw.

was chosen for you, today you can choose the "self" you want to be.

The Christian view of identity differs from both the traditional view (we receive our identity from our community) and the modern view (we form our identity through self-exploration). We believe our identity is conferred upon us by our Creator, God. *In other words, we won't find our truest definition of self by looking out or in, but by looking up.*

Yes, God has a set of beliefs about you. We will talk in more detail about what those beliefs are, but the goal of this book is to help you align your beliefs about yourself with God's beliefs about you. If you see yourself the way God sees you, you will have the truest picture of who you are, thereby giving you the peace, security, humility, courage, and confidence to live into your created ideal.

Who is God and why does he get to tell me who I am?

Let's back up a bit and talk about why God's opinion of you is the only one that matters. The source of almost all the information we receive about God is the Bible, so I will be referring to Scripture often. If you don't trust that the Bible is God's words to us, written down by men under the inspiration of the Holy Spirit, please keep reading, but be aware that I write from that foundational perspective.

There are many attributes of God in the pages of Scripture, but I want to focus on just a few of them as they relate to our discussion of identity. First, God is *self-sufficient and self-existent*. The name God chose for himself when he revealed himself to his people through Moses was *I AM*.[16] His mere existence was enough to engender the respect of all people and the trust of his special people. Colossians 1 tells us that God "is before all things, and in him all things hold together."[17] Why is it important to understand this about God? Because, unlike humans, God has no needs. He doesn't need humans to stroke his ego or fulfill his desire for connection. He doesn't need us to authenticate or justify his identity. He simply *is*.

Second, God is *Creator*. Going back to Colossians 1, "For by him all things were created: the things in heaven and on earth, visible and invisible, whether thrones or powers or rulers or authorities; all things were created by him and for him."[18] God being the Creator has many ramifications for us as his creation. First, the "earth is the Lord's and everything in it."[19] He made it, he owns it. Second, "God reigns over the nations."[20] He made it, he rules it. Third, and most relevant to our study of identity, "God understands the way to [wisdom], and he alone knows where it dwells, for he views the ends of the earth and sees everything under the heavens."[21] He made it, he understands it. He wrote the owner's manual for everything he made. Since he knows how we were designed to work, we can trust him when he tells us who we are and how we should live.

Lastly, God is *Love*.[22] We have determined that God, in his power, created the universe. He didn't

---

[16] Exodus 3:13–14
[17] Colossians 1:17
[18] Colossians 1:16
[19] Psalm 24:1
[20] Psalm 47:8
[21] Job 28:23–24
[22] 1 John 4:16

need to create anything in order to prove his existence. So why did he create? Because he is, in essence, love. Everything that pours out from him is done by love, for love, and in love. It is critical to our understanding of human identity that we get this aspect of God right. He loves his creation. Peter Kreeft, in his book *The God Who Loves You*, writes this about the love of God as the motivation for creation:

> Why did God create? He needed nothing, being perfect and eternal. There is only one possible motive: altruistic love, sheer generosity, the desire to share His goodness and glory with others.[23]

God doesn't just love his creation in a general sense, like I love the Seahawks, U2, and chocolate chip cookies. No, God intimately loves each individual he created, including you.

> God is a person, and the only way to understand a person is by love, and the only way to perfect understanding is by perfect love . . . The genius may know more things about you, but only the lover knows you, for genius knows things, but love knows persons.[24]

In order to trust that what God says about your identity is true and reliable and to live according to his design, you must believe not only that he is pow-

---

[23] Peter Kreeft, *The God Who Loves You* (San Francisco: Ignatius Press, 2004), 44.
[24] Kreeft, *The God Who Loves You*, 33.

erful and wise but also that he loves you deeply and has your best interest at heart.

Next, let's dig into what God believes about you.

Reflection Questions

1. Have you experienced the anxiety that comes with the quest to "find yourself" or "be who you want to be"? How can allowing God to define your identity actually provide freedom *from* this anxiety? What might you be free *to* do or be?

2. What are some of the ways you might be striving to define yourself?

3. How does understanding God as a self-sufficient, loving Creator help you to trust in the identity he gives you?

2

WHAT DOES GOD BELIEVE ABOUT YOU?

My frame was not hidden from you, when I was being made in secret, intricately woven in the depths of the earth. Your eyes saw my unformed substance; in your book were written, every one of them, the days that were formed for me, when as yet there was none of them.

– Psalm 139:15–16

The end, then, of learning is to repair the ruins of our first parents by regaining to know God aright, and out of that knowledge to love him, to imitate him, to be like him, as we may the nearest by possessing our souls of true virtue, which being united to the heavenly grace of faith makes up the highest perfection.

– John Milton[1]

I n Genesis, we learn God's original plan for the human race and who he envisioned us to be.

---

[1] John Milton, *Milton's Tractate on Education* (Cambridge: University Press, 1905), Chapter 1, Kindle Edition.

The Genesis of Identity

Take a minute right now to read the first two chapters of the Bible. Genesis 1 is the fly-by version of creation while Genesis 2 is the more detailed version. In Genesis 1:27, we read "God created man in his own image. In the image of God he created him;[2] male and female he created them."

Unlike the oceans, land, trees, shrubs, animals, and everything else God had created up to this point, *man* (and this is the Hebrew word *adam,* which means mankind, or humankind, not just the male gender) was created in God's image. There's a fancy Latin phrase for this, which you might have heard before: *Imago Dei.* This concept of being created in God's image is pregnant with meaning, but for our study we'll focus specifically on the answers to the questions "Who am I?" and "Why am I here?"

Who am I?

The Imago Dei explains who we are in a poignant way. God could have chosen to make us look like anything, but he chose to make us look like himself. We are not little gods (we were formed from dirt after all), but we have dignity, value, and worth because we were made to look and act like our Father. We are always telling kids how much they look or act like their parents or grandparents. "You have your mom's smile." "You have your dad's temperament." "You got your musical ability from your grandmother." We're always drawing similarities and connecting the DNA

---

[2] Many versions say "him," but the correct translation is "them."

dots. It gives us comfort and stability to know where we came from, even if where we came from isn't all that great. Adopted children sometimes struggle with this lack of history, and many find the need to search out their birth parents so they can feel rooted. God's making us in his image means that we are connected to him, almost like our DNA connects us to our parents.

The Imago Dei not only gives us dignity, value, and worth, but it also gives us a unique status. We are God's special handiwork. Unlike the rest of creation, which he spoke into being, God picked up some dirt from the ground and added water to make clay. With his hands, he carefully molded it into a body and breathed into that body the breath of life. It was an intimate, painstaking work, but in the end he stepped back and declared, "It is very good."[3] It was very good because it was in his image! We were sculpted and proudly signed by the Master Artist.

Why am I here?

The Imago Dei answers the question "Who am I?" (or maybe more appropriately "*Whose* am I?") by giving us dignity, value, and worth. The Imago Dei also answers the question, "Why am I here?" It gives us purpose. If God made us in his image, then he must have meant for us to look and act like him, right? He wouldn't have made us in his image and then said, "Now you can be or do whatever your heart pleases." In all the instructions God gave the original humans about multiplying and subduing the earth, the idea was that they were supposed to *be like him*. In the

---

[3] Genesis 1:31

same way he created the earth, we are to recreate (or procreate). We are to multiply his image across the globe not only through birthing babies, but also by helping bring people into new birth in Christ. In the same way he created order from chaos, we are to bring order to our world. In other words, God designed the first humans to *imitate* him.[4]

He also designed us to *represent* him. In the Roman Empire, the emperor's face was stamped onto the coinage as a symbol of territorial control. Every time you looked at a denarii and saw Caesar's face, you were reminded that he was in control. The coin wasn't the emperor, but it bore his image. We are stamped with God's image for the exact same reason. We are walking denarii—ambassadors of God to this world.[5] Adam and Eve were, in essence, the proxy for God in the Garden. They were conduits of his love to each other and their world.

Lastly, being made in the Imago Dei means we have a responsibility to *glorify* God on this earth. This basically means we humble ourselves in order to make a big deal out of God. We are to walk this earth perpetually aware that we are not our own little gods; rather, we were created by God in his image and for his purpose. This knowledge should cause us to see ourselves as putty in the Sculptor's hands. It should encourage us to place ultimate trust in God's plan for our lives. It should also help us see our talents and abilities not as our own to do with as we please but as gifts given to us in order to uniquely glorify our Creator.[6]

---

4 Ephesians 5:1
5 2 Corinthians 5:20
6 Psalm 86:12

What Went Wrong?

Adam and Eve did not have an identity crisis. They didn't actually have an identity apart from God until the Fall. If you remember from the last chapter, the word identity comes from the root *idem*, which means sameness or mirror image. When Adam and Eve looked in the mirror, they didn't see themselves, they saw God. In a sense, they themselves were mirrors. God's glory shone down on them, and they reflected it back to him and to the world around them.

When I used to watch Snow White with my girls, I had to fight the urge to shout, "Don't eat that apple!" which of course went unheeded time after time. The same thing happens when I read Genesis 3. I wish I could stop what happens next. The disobedience of Adam and Eve put a curse on mankind that complicated and muddied our identity as humans. Now, instead of seeing God when we look in the mirror, we see ourselves. Instead of reflecting God's glory to the world around us, we either glorify ourselves (pride) or we denigrate ourselves (shame). We are shadows of our former selves and we don't even know it. We seek identity in everything except the one place where we will find it: in the God who created us.

A New Identity

All is not lost, however. "In the fullness of time, God sent his Son."[7] God sent us something better than a representative from heaven. He sent his own Son, God in human form. Jesus came not only to perfectly imitate, represent, and glorify God on earth (tasks

---

[7] Galatians 4:4

that Adam could not accomplish), but also to give up his very life in order to give us a new identity.

Consider this illustration. You are in a cold courtroom, standing trial for multiple infractions of the law. You plead guilty to the lengthy list of charges brought against you. After deliberating for only an hour, the jury foreman dispassionately reads the verdict: guilty of all charges. The sentencing phase is next, but the judge needs no time deciding your fate. Unlike the jury foreman, though, the judge seems genuinely sorrowful as he reads the death sentence, which is the only just penalty afforded by law. At the last syllable of the last word of his sad proclamation, a man in white slams open the heavy courtroom doors and runs down the aisle shouting something to the judge. The judge recognizes this man.

"Son, what is the matter?"

"I want to take the sentence of this man upon myself, but on one condition."

"What's that?"

"I want his record wiped clean, and I want the court to reverse his guilty verdict."

"Why should I do that?" asks the judge.

"Because *I* am not guilty," the man answers. "I have led a perfect life, and I want you to replace the charges against this person with my blank record. I want to take those charges on myself and suffer the penalty for his crimes."

The judge looks down at you and asks, "Do you want to pay for your crimes, or do you want this perfect representative to assume your debt?"

In faith, believing that your surrogate will do as he says, you hold out your hands to the guard to unlock your handcuffs. You tearfully sign the paperwork transferring your guilt and punishment to the man in white, and then you get the biggest surprise of all. The judge takes off his robe, steps down from the bench, gives you a huge hug, and gives you more paperwork to sign. Adoption paperwork. Dazed and elated, you stagger out of the courtroom with a new identity—the child of the judge.

This parable deals with three important aspects of your salvation as it pertains to your identity. First, you were *forgiven*.[8] You deserved punishment, but Jesus took it for you. This is a crucial piece to understanding who you are, but it is only the first step. Second, you were *justified*, meaning your record was expunged.[9] Too many Christians stop at forgiveness. They can't really believe God sees a clean record when he looks at them. Third, as if forgiveness and justification weren't enough, you were *adopted*.[10] You are not merely tolerated as a charity case. You are not an employee, working hard to earn the boss's approval. You are not a peasant who gets the lucky ticket to the coronation ball but must stand in the back or sit in the rafters. No, you are the guest of honor, the son or daughter of the King.

In Romans, God inspired Paul to clearly and repeatedly affirm not only our forgiveness but also our justification and our adoption. After the first seven chapters of attorney-esque arguments, Paul builds to the emotional crescendo in Romans 8: "Therefore there is now NO condemnation to those who are in Christ Jesus!"[11]

---

[8] John 3:16
[9] Romans 3–4
[10] 1 John 3:1
[11] Romans 8:1, emphasis added

Paul, in Colossians 3, uses another phrase I have always loved when describing our new identity. He says in verse three, "For you died, and your life is now hidden with Christ in God."[12] Being *hidden with Christ* conjures up the image of Father Christmas in Dickens's *A Christmas Carol* hiding two children (Ignorance and Want) under his massive green robe. It also reminds me of *The Hiding Place* by Corrie ten Boom, when the SS come searching for Jews, but they are well-hidden in a secret apartment concealed by bookcases. The piercing spotlight of God's perfect standard of righteousness is still shining on us, but we are safely hidden under the robe or behind the bookcase. When God looks at us, he cannot find us. He can only see his perfect Son who is shielding us from his justice.

Sanctification

While we cannot be condemned for our sins once we have laid them on Christ, that doesn't mean God sits back and lets us be controlled by our sinful passions. He cares too much about us to let us self-destruct. Remember, he holds the blueprints to our lives. He knows how we were designed to live and what will give us the most joy and fulfillment. That is why he gave us the gift of the Holy Spirit when we were adopted into his family. If we are hidden behind Christ and shielded from God's view, we are fully exposed to the Holy Spirit, who sees our mess and conforms us into Christ's image. C.S. Lewis puts it this way in *Mere Christianity*:

---

[12] Colossians 3:3

Now the whole offer which Christianity makes is this: that we can, if we let God have His way, come to share in the life of Christ . . . Christ is the Son of God. If we share in this kind of life we also shall be sons of God. We shall love the Father as He does and the Holy Ghost will arise in us . . . Every Christian is to become a little Christ. The whole purpose of becoming a Christian is simply nothing else.[13]

Picture in your mind God the Father on the left, looking at his perfect Son, Jesus. You are huddled, disfigured, and lame—cocooned, if you will—in Jesus, safely out of God's sight. The Holy Spirit is in the cocoon with you. He still does not condemn you; otherwise the Trinity would not have unity of mind. But, he gets to work right away, healing your lameness and re-forming your disfigurement until slowly and steadily you are conformed to the beautiful image of Christ who is in you and you in him. The longer you are a Christian, and the more you surrender and cooperate with God's Spirit, the more you should look like the perfect Jesus that God sees. On this side of heaven you will never attain that perfection, but it should give you great hope to know that God is at work in you, refining and chiseling you into the Imago Dei he already sees in you.

And we all, who with unveiled faces contemplate the Lord's glory, are being transformed into his

---

13 C.S. Lewis, *Mere Christianity* (New York: MacMillan Publishing Company, 1952), 137–138.

image with ever-increasing glory, which comes from the Lord, who is the Spirit.[14]

This is what God believes about you

Let's summarize everything we've discussed so far:

1. Your identity is what you believe to be true about yourself. It informs your emotions and motivates your actions.
2. You do not receive your identity from your community and you will not find it by looking within yourself. God confers upon you your identity, and your life-long pursuit is to bring your beliefs about yourself into alignment with God's beliefs about you.
3. What is your purpose? You were created and designed to imitate, represent, and glorify him.
4. Due to the failure of our first parents, you were born with handicaps that, apart from God's grace, make it impossible for you to live how you were designed.
5. God has made it possible for him to see you the way he saw Adam and Eve before they sinned, and that is through the sacrifice of his perfect Son. Now, when he looks at you he sees the original Imago Dei. He sees this not because you are perfect but because Jesus is blocking his view.

---

[14] 2 Corinthians 3:18

If God believes all this about me, then this is my identity. I was born a sinner, incapable of living out my created ideal, but Jesus stepped in front of me, "bore the wrath reserved for me,"[15] and now God only sees Jesus when he looks at me.

> *I was a condemned criminal in God's court, but now I am a forgiven, blameless, and beloved child of God.*

The first half of this statement is important because you must never forget you have been rescued. Pride cannot enter your identity when you remember that everything you are is due to God's grace. The second half of this statement gives you value, security, and confidence because your identity is fixed and immovable. Failure doesn't remove it. Loss can't change it. People have no control over it.

---

[15] "All I Have is Christ," Jordan Kauflin, *Sovereign Grace Music*, 2008, http://sovereigngracemusic.org/music/songs/all-i-have-is-christ/.

Reflection Questions

1. Knowing we were created in the Imago Dei should have significant bearing on our *being* and *doing*. What are some "I am" statements that frequent your thoughts and also run counter to the dignity, value, and worth of being made in God's image? What are some of your frequent "I should" statements that run counter to your created purpose to imitate, represent, and glorify God?

2. Having a common value and purpose with all of humanity does not in any way diminish your uniqueness. What are some ways God has specially gifted *you* to imitate, represent, and glorify him on this earth?

3. When you trust Christ to be your perfect replacement, God says you are forgiven, justified, and adopted. Which of these amazing gifts is most difficult for you to receive? Why?

3

WHAT IS THE GOAL?

For many of us, the problem is not that we think poorly about ourselves. The problem is that we can't stop thinking about ourselves.

– Sharon Hodde Miller[1]

Dear friends, since God so loved us, we also ought to love one another. No one has ever seen God; but if we love one another, God lives in us and his love is made complete in us.

– 1 John 4:11–12

R emember in chapter one when I said that a correct understanding of your God-given identity is the key to leading a life of peace, security, humility, courage, and confidence? You might be wondering how just changing what you believe about yourself can accomplish all of this.

I've heard it said that if you want to change any thought or behavior, you have to start with correct *theology.* This is what you believe about God, and we covered this in chapter one. Once you have a right theology, you must apply good *anthropology.* This is what you believe about humanity, which we dis-cussed in chapter two when we talked about our

---

[1] Sharon Miller, *Free of Me: Why Life is Better When It's Not About You* (Grand Rapids: Baker Books, 2017), 37.

created purpose, how we got off track, and the restoration of the Imago Dei that we can experience after salvation. Finally, you must address *sociology*. This is what you believe about and how you treat other people, which is what we will tackle in this chapter. This is where the rubber meets the road. This is where having a firm grasp of your identity actually makes a difference in your day-to-day life.

The end goal of all of this identity talk is not to leave you feeling better about yourself. The end goal is to use your identity in Christ as the foundation upon which to build a life that is not about you at all. You are merely a vehicle, propelled by Christ's love and acceptance to love and serve the world. Remember that your created purpose is to imitate, represent, and glorify God here on earth. And what is God's driving motivation, his every action, his very essence and character? It is love (John 4:16). Love is our target. Jesus said as much when he whittled down all the commandments into two: love God and love your neighbor.[2]

So, how does understanding your identity (seeing yourself the way God sees you) help you love God and love your neighbor? Understanding your identity in Christ allows you to accept yourself and then forget yourself, thus setting you free to love the way God loves.

Self-Acceptance

When you begin believing the same things about yourself that God believes about you, you will come to a place of self-acceptance. I hear this basic

---

[2] Luke 10:27

statement from so many Christians: "It's great to believe that God accepts you, but it's dangerous to
believe that you should accept yourself." I used to
think this way, but now it seems ludicrous to me.
How can you say God accepts you and then go on to
say it is unacceptable to accept yourself? The people
who perpetually self-critique and self-flagellate are
the ones who deep-down don't believe they've been
fully accepted and justified by Christ. They believe
God is somehow displeased with them.

I can almost hear the "buts" shouting at me
through the pages. "But if I accept myself, won't I be
accepting the bad as well as the good?" "But if I accept
myself, am I not condoning the sin I know still lurks
in my heart?" "But self-acceptance is really just giving
up the fight, right?"

Self-acceptance is not tolerance of sinful behavior, nor is it giving up. Self-acceptance can and
should be the freedom you need in order to work on
your most stubborn, rough edges. If I see myself as
perfectly right in God's eyes, I no longer fear his
wrathful punishment. If I see myself as fully loved by
God, I no longer strive to earn his favor. When I succeed in my mission to love and act like Jesus, I am
grateful. But when I fail, I do not doubt for one second
that God's approval has been removed from my life. I
do not get stuck in shame. Rather, I am able to separate my identity from my action, ask for forgiveness,
then get up and keep trying, in perfect confidence of
Christ's love for me.

Life as a disciple of Jesus should be a paradox of
self-acceptance and self-improvement. I accept myself with all my flaws because God delights in me with
all my flaws. However, I improve myself because being

loved fully motivates me to love better. I am now striving to love God and others better, not for the
acceptance of the One I love but as a reflection of the
One whose love is changing me.

Labels are important. Did you know behavioral
psychologists are moving away from the "disorder" labels they once doled out for every harmful behavior?
The new and improved thinking is that if you are labeled with a disorder, you are more likely to believe
you have no hope for change. Instead of saying, for
example, "You have obsessive compulsive disorder,"
psychologists have moved to saying, "You are ob-
sessing right now. Let's try to figure out why and help
you to obsess less." The patient then gets busy working on his behavior patterns. This approach allows
many to achieve long-lasting change.

If you placed your faith in Jesus, your label has
changed. Paul calls us "new creatures."[3] Whereas you
were once a *sinner* who did some good things, you are
now a *saint* who still sins sometimes.[4] You may think
this is a minor parsing of terms, but changing your
label changes everything. Understanding your change
in state impacts how resilient you are when you sin,
how you treat other Christians when they sin against
you, your ability to hope for change, and your ability
to receive criticism. If you are a believer in Christ, you
are not a sinner. You are a saint.

Self-Forgetfulness

When you begin believing the same things about
yourself that God believes about you, you will

---

[3] 2 Corinthians 5:17
[4] Colossians 1:12

experience more self-forgetfulness. Why? Because you understand it is only by God's grace you have been forgiven, justified, and adopted! You did absolutely nothing to deserve the new label of "saint."

The term "self-forgetfulness" comes from C.S. Lewis's chapter on humility in *Mere Christianity.* He writes that when you meet a truly humble person, "all you will think about him is that he seemed a cheerful, intelligent chap who took a real interest in what *you* said to *him* . . . He will not be thinking about humility: he will not be thinking about himself at all."[5]

Self-forgetfulness goes a step further than humility. Humility is having the right perspective of yourself as small, weak, and undeserving in comparison to the majesty, glory, and perfection of Almighty God. But if we stop there, we might tend more toward self-loathing, which would still be thinking too much about ourselves. The point is to find your truest self in the mirror of God's love and acceptance, then forget yourself in pursuit of loving God and others.

When you are firmly rooted in your identity as a beloved child of God, you will no longer need affirmation from fellow humans. You can recognize your inherent value, and you can be free to love others whether they affirm you or not. We'll talk more about this in further chapters, but here are some more benefits of living a life of self-forgetfulness:

- The ability to see criticism as helpful correction rather than an assault on your identity

---

[5] C.S. Lewis, *Mere Christianity* (New York: MacMillan Publishing Company, 1952), 99.

- The ability to admit weaknesses, to apologize for failures, and to laugh at yourself
- The ability to see past others' assaults and recognize that they often stem from being wounded
- The ability to take a compliment without attaching it to your identity
- The ability to give up trying to control other people or circumstances
- The ability to shed anxiety over your performance
- The ability to serve and love the "least of these" with no praise except the all-seeing smile of the Father

This sounds like a dream, doesn't it? It is exhausting to be thinking about yourself all the time. C.S. Lewis calls self-forgetfulness "the infinite relief of having for once got rid of all the silly nonsense about your own dignity which has made you restless and unhappy all your life."[6]

Freedom

Seeing yourself the way God sees you is the only way to move forward in pursuit of living out your created ideal. When you settle into your identity as a beloved child of God, you will deal a death blow to shame and pride, replacing them with self-acceptance and self-forgetfulness. When I consider how this change of perspective has altered my life, the one word that comes to mind is *freedom*. It is both a freedom *from* and a freedom *to*. When I am free from self-loathing,

---

[6] Lewis, *Mere Christianity*, 99.

self-criticism, self-promotion, self-righteousness, and self-protection, I am free to love God and others. A basketball player doesn't train for months, discipline himself to eat properly, and spend copious amounts of time in the gym just to be free from self-indulgence. No, he frees himself *from* self-indulgence in order to be free *to* compete in the sport he loves. A professional musician practices for years of her life, freeing herself *from* the restraints of technique so she can be free *to* perform with expression and emotion.

It is hard work to retrain your heart and mind to be free from the identity chains that bind you. It will be hard for some of you to work through this book and uncover the identity lies that are at the root of many of your habitual thoughts and practices. But just think about what you will be free to do once those chains have been loosed! You will be free to fail without condemnation, to try again without cynicism, to serve without thanks, to give without strings, and to love without fear.

When the kids were little, one of my favorite books to read to them was Max Lucado's *You Are Special.*[7] The characters in the story carved wooden dolls, the Wemmicks, who live in a village where their social status is determined by dots and stars applied by their peers. If a Wemmick stuck a star sticker on a friend, that meant she had done something to earn their approval, like performing well or being beautiful. Likewise, dot stickers meant they had not measured up. Of course, the Wemmicks with the most stars were on the highest rungs of the social ladder, while the dot-laden dolls were on the lowest rungs. The

---

[7] Max Lucado, *You are Special* (Wheaton: Crossway Publishing, 1997).

main character, a very average Punchinello, was sad and frustrated by his dot-to-star ratio.

One day, he met Lucia. He noticed right away that she had neither dots nor stars. As she interacted with her fellow Wemmicks, they tried to stick stars and dots on her, but the stickers instantly fluttered to the ground. Punchinello was intrigued. She seemed to move through life with a joy and freedom he had never possessed or seen in his fellow dolls. He had to know Lucia's secret, so he finally gathered the courage to ask. Her answer was not what Punchinello expected.

The secret, she told Punchinello, was to simply spend time every day with the woodcarver, Eli. Feeling very small and embarrassed by his dots, Punchinello entered the woodcarver's shop one day. To his surprise, Eli was not fearsome and intimidating but kind and loving. He assured Punchinello that he had made him exactly how he wanted. He told him he was pleased with him, no matter what his fellow ' Wemmicks said. Eli invited Punchinello to spend time in his shop every day to begin to understand his value. Bolstered by the love and acceptance of the woodcarver, Punchinello left the shop, and as he did a dot from his shoulder fell to the ground.

Like Punchinello, we are created, loved, and accepted despite (and even because of) our imperfections. Our woodcarver sees past the stars and dots that mean so much to us, all the way to the inherent Imago Dei within. Like Eli did with Punchinello, God invites us to spend time with him to learn how to see ourselves the way he sees us. We might be surprised to learn that rather than frowning with displeasure, he smiles when we trip up and our ego gets the better of us. He lavishes us with extravagant grace, allowing us time and space to grow into maturity. He parents us with patience and affection, offering correction when we fail, comfort when we hurt, encouragement when we doubt, and guidance when we lose our way. With the assurance that we are fully loved, we can be like Lucia, free from self-doubt and self-promotion. We can be free to blossom into the people God created us to be.

Reflection Questions

1. Have you struggled to fully accept yourself with all your limitations and flaws? How might you see those flaws differently if you could accept yourself the way Christ accepts you?

2. How is self-forgetfulness different from diminishing or erasing the self? Look back at the list of benefits from living a self-forgetful life. Which one is the most appealing to you? Would you add any?

3. Freedom is most often found at the end of a long road of hard work. What work do you perceive lies ahead of you in your desire to be free of self?

4

YOUR STORY

Heaven and I wept together, and its sweet tears
were salt with mortal mine.

– Francis Thompson[1]

The bars of life at which we fret,
That seem to prison and control,
Are but the doors of daring, set
Ajar before the soul.

– Henry van Dyke[2]

I
n the first three chapters of this book we discussed who we were created to be, why we
struggle to fulfill our created calling, and how
finding our identity in Christ is the only way to find
self-acceptance, self-forgetfulness, and freedom. It
seems like a fairly easy formula for success, right?
Wrong. Identity issues run deep. The rest of this book
deals with how to uncover the root causes of identity
misplacement and how Jesus can redeem your story
by helping you see it through his lens. But before we
dive into all of that, we have to know what we're up

---

[1] Francis Thompson, *The Hound of Heaven* from *A Treasury of the World's Best-Loved Poems* (New York: Avenel Books, 1961), 168.
[2] Henry van Dyke, *Doors of Daring* from *The Book of Virtues* (New York: Simon and Schuster, 1993), 480.

against. We have three main enemies that keep us from believing the truth about our God-given identity.

Sin

The first enemy we encounter in our desire to live out our created ideal is sin. I say the first because the Bible says we are literally born with a bent toward sin.[3] C.S. Lewis said, "The moment you have a self at all, there is a possibility of putting yourself first— wanting to be the centre—wanting to be God, in fact."[4] This tendency to want to be our own god is the essence of the sin nature. It is what motivated Lucifer to rebel against God and our first parents to disobey God in the Garden. This rebellious spirit is woven into the DNA strands of every human born since the Fall— with the exception of the God-man, Jesus.

Why is it important to remember this enemy of the sin nature in your quest to live out your God-given identity? Because merely solidifying your identity will not take away every temptation to fulfill your sinful desires. This book might help you to discover the motivation behind your habitual sin patterns, and I hope and pray you will gain victory over them. Keep in mind, however, that your battle with sin will be a life-long process. Paul talked about this in Romans 7:20: "Now if I do what I do not want to do, it is no longer I who do it, but it is sin living in me that does it." In all of our discussion about the formation of identity, we need to remember that we are not simply the product of our environment. We were born with a self-centered

---

[3] Psalm 51:5
[4] C.S. Lewis, *Mere Christianity* (New York: MacMillan Publishing Company, 1952), 38.

sin nature, and the environment we were raised in simply capitalized on the handicaps we received from our first parents, Adam and Eve.

You might be thinking, "Wait a minute. I thought you just finished telling us that we are not sinners, but saints." We were *born* sinners, separated from God. Once we placed our faith in Jesus's substitution for the penalty of our sin, God ripped off our "sinner" label and exchanged it for "saint." What he did not remove from us was our sinful desires (I wish!). We are saints who still have sinful tendencies. But, as we discussed in chapter two, he did give us a new and powerful weapon in our fight—the Holy Spirit. One of the primary roles of the Holy Spirit in a believer's life is to convict them of sin and then give them the power to change.[5]

Satan

Not only do we have to contend with our sin nature but we also have another real though unseen enemy who wants nothing more than to keep us from living how we were created to live. I realize it's not popular to talk about this enemy, but since his presence and power are verified by Scripture, we would be wise not to ignore him. Satan's end goal is to defeat God's grand and glorious plan of bringing all things back into harmony with himself. *We* know how the story will end—with Satan's ultimate defeat and demise—but I'm not sure *he* knows he will be defeated. Even if he does, he is not going down without a fight. Satan's main strategy is to win over the hearts and minds of

---

[5] Romans 8

the humans God created.[6] Just as the serpent planted doubts in Eve's mind about the goodness of God, Satan uses our minds as the primary medium for his manipulative tactics. This is why Scripture is full of admonishment to let the Spirit "govern your mind,"[7] to "be transformed by the renewing of your mind,"[8] to "take captive every thought to make it obedient to Christ,"[9] to "be alert and sober-minded" as a defense against the devil's schemes,[10] and to think about "excellent, praiseworthy, right, pure, noble, and lovely things."[11]

The mind is Satan's battlefield, but what are his tactics? He will use whatever strategy is necessary to defeat you, but he does have some go-to maneuvers. The first is deception. The Bible says Satan is the "Father of lies."[12] He is the master manipulator, throwing in enough truth to make his lies plausible and working hard to keep the veil of deceit from lifting. When it comes to identity issues, Satan does not want you to believe the truth about who you are in God's sight. As you start down the path of uncovering his lies, he will be fighting tooth and nail to keep you from replacing them with the truth he knows will set you free.

A second trick Satan uses is shame. Satan has actually been given the name "Accuser" in several places throughout Scripture. Revelation 12:10 says Satan hurls accusations about the saints "before our

---

[6] Ephesians 6:12
[7] Romans 8:6
[8] Romans 12:2
[9] 2 Corinthians 10:5
[10] 1 Peter 5:8
[11] Philippians 4:8
[12] John 8:44

God day and night." Thankfully, none of those accusations are entertained by God because they have already been laid on Christ. Satan not only accuses us to God, but he also accuses us to ourselves. He knows guilt and shame are heavy weights that will sideline you from the race. If he can convince you that your past sin defines you, then he wins. Even if you spend eternity in heaven, Satan has won a major victory if he has effectively filled your running shoes with the cement of shame.

Story

And now for the third enemy: your story. Because we live in a fallen world inhabited by sinful people and informed by the "ruler of the kingdom of the air"[13] (Satan), your story has not always been easy. The reality is many of us have pages filled with heartbreak, abandonment, loss, abuse, betrayal, failure, poverty, and disappointment. Hopefully you've had chapters of joy, beauty, and love too, but there is no denying the experiences in your life have shaped your identity in deep and powerful ways. The rest of this book will help you flip back through the pages of your story to discover the foundational identity falsehoods that were sown when you were young. Then, with the help of Scripture and the power of the Holy Spirit, you will be able to uproot those lies and continue writing your narrative.

This isn't some kind of revisionist therapy. You can't go back and *rewrite* your story or just pretend those bad things didn't happen to you. Those hurts leave permanent marks on your soul. However, you

---

[13] Ephesians 2:2

can allow God to *redeem* your story by letting him heal the identity wounds of your past and give you a new lens through which to read your story: the lens of his perfect love.

Why Go Back?

To illustrate the necessity of dredging up the identity lies from your past, I'm going to share with you one of the most embarrassing but pivotal growth moments in my story.

Several years ago, a friend and I were put in charge of the teaching sessions for pastors' wives at a church planting conference. For months we met, asking ourselves, "What would we have wanted to know before we began the journey of church planting?" We planned our sessions, prayed about who we would ask to teach, and decided how to best use the short time we were allotted. One week before the conference, I woke up to an email in my inbox from the president of our church planting network. The email expressed sudden disapproval from the pastor's wife of the church where the conference would be hosted. Even though she had never expressed interest in being on the teaching team, she was hurt we didn't ask her to teach and wanted us to change our plans to include her.

Let me pause here to share with you what was riding on the line for me emotionally at the time. Not only was this my first time leading these sessions and I wanted to make a good impression, but I looked up to this woman. A lot. We had a sort-of friendship. I really cared what she thought of me. I hadn't meant to hurt her. I had heard through the grapevine she was not interested in teaching. But if she did want to teach, why did she wait until the last minute to speak up? Why did she feel like she had to go through the president of the organization and not come directly to me? She had my email address and my phone number. I couldn't bear to think she had misunderstood my intentions and thought the worst of me. To make matters worse, she did not give me the opportunity to apologize and make things right. I emailed her a long apology, as well as an explanation of my reasoning, but I never heard directly from her. Instead, the president relayed her hurt to me over the phone and asked us to give up some of our time so she could lead a session.

You can guess how this made me feel with so much of my pride at stake. I was crushed. I was angry. I cried. I yelled out my frustrations to my husband and to God. I carried on conversations with her in my head, defending myself and begging her forgiveness. For days I fretted, losing sleep and feeling sick to my stomach. Looking back now, I'm embarrassed by how desperately I had been craving her approval. Even while I was in the throes of humiliation, I berated myself for letting it get to me as much as it did. I asked myself, "Would I have reacted so strongly if I had been hurt by someone who I didn't care to impress?" The answer was a big fat no.

I've since moved on and I've softened my heart toward her, even though we've never spoken. I share this story not to bring up old grievances with this person but to show you the condition of my heart at the time.

The Identity Lie

There are two ways to look at this humbling chapter in my story. The first was my conditioned response, which was to chalk it up to my sinful nature. I could see this as another opportunity for God to reveal the ugliness of my prideful heart and chip away at the idols there. That was most certainly true. I needed to see how much work was still to be done with my recurring sins of pride and people pleasing. The second way of thinking about it did not come until years later when I began studying identity. As I reevaluated my story, I realized one of the reasons I reacted so severely to this woman's dismissal of me was that I still carried the identity from my childhood as "the good, responsible girl who does not let people down, especially people in authority." I could not handle her believing I was anything but good because, if she did, I felt I would somehow lose a part of my identity.

Self-Acceptance

When I dug deeper into my story to discover which identity foundation stones these flashes of emotion originated from, two things happened. First, I was able to stop berating myself so much and instead offer myself a little grace and acceptance. Not a free pass, mind you. I was still on the hook for my sinful reaction. But now I could see that I was reacting that way not just because of my evil heart but because of the threat to my identity. This helped me to fan away the smoke of guilt so I could deal with the root issue. Unhindered by guilt and shame, I was able to dig up the false identity of "the good, responsible girl who doesn't let people down" and replace it with "the fully loved and accepted daughter of God, who will disappoint people, but who will never lose the approval of my heavenly Father."

Self-Forgetfulness

Second, doing the hard work of digging down to the identity lies that fueled my sinful reaction and replacing them with God's truth about me led me from self-acceptance to self-forgetfulness. Armed with the reassurance that God was pleased with me, I began to lose my need for people's affirmation. You see, just acknowledging my sin and confessing it didn't help me to forget myself. I still struggled with wanting to present my best self and impress the people in my life I respected most. However, going back and letting God redeem my story did the trick! When I went back to little girl Christy and convinced her that her value wasn't in people's approval but in her position as beloved daughter of God, my adult heart began to transform. Slowly, I began to care less about impressing people and began to see myself as loved and valued by my Creator. I had nothing to prove and I could get on with the business of loving the people God gave me to love.

Freedom

Third, something unexpected started happening. The real me, the one I had tried to shield from public view, began to peek out from behind the carefully-crafted curtain of perfection I had been sewing since childhood. I began to show people my process in real time, rather than waiting to show them the finished product (as if any part of me is ever a "finished product"). Since I had nothing to prove, I could reveal the true me, warts and all, without worrying that people might not like what they see. I was free to carry the real me into every situation without feeling like I needed to wear a mask. And I was amazed and happy to learn that most people actually like the real version of me better than the perfect version. Go figure.

So, here is the short answer to the question, "Why go back?" Going back is the only path to real, lasting change. Simply dealing with your sinful behaviors without digging down to the core motives of your heart is like chopping the head off a weed without pulling up the root.

Isn't This All Just a Blame Game?

Psychotherapy critics have said there is little to no value in dredging up your past and exploring your "inner child." They say this can become a crutch for people who need someone other than themselves to blame for their bad behavior ("I am mean to people because my mom was mean to me").

I can understand this criticism, especially when the therapy is not rooted in a Christian perspective. Just having empathy for your childhood trauma will not help you change your current thoughts and actions. Blame-shifting will never provide a permanent solution to your habitual sin. However, understanding that some of your attitudes and behaviors have their roots in childhood experiences is an indispensable tool in helping you to change those behaviors. If, for example, you understand that your tendency to lash out at people comes from being lashed out at as a child, you can apply the balm of God's truth to that original wound. When your wound is bound up and healed, you no longer feel the need to live as the wounded one but as God's beloved instead. This kind of deep healing is what brings lasting change. Just piling on the guilt over each individual offense without tracing those offenses back to their source can be ineffective and frustrating. The goal is to overcome those behaviors in order to love God and others.

The Shaping of Identity

What were the letters, words, and paragraphs that were woven together to create your story? Which experiences from your past contributed to the shaping of your current self? The second half of this book will deal with the three aspects of your environment that I believe might have had the biggest impact on the formation of your identity. They are:

1. The parental *love* you received
2. The *tribes* you belonged to
3. The *voices* you listened to

In each case, we will discover the ways in which God's love, his tribes, and his voice can give you the ability to believe that what he says about you is true. Identifying the lies you believe and where they came from is the first step toward changing your identity. The next step is learning and believing the truth.

Remember

As you go back and read through the chapters of your life, keep in mind that your Creator is the only one who can give you your true identity. It might help to read this Psalm aloud as a prayer to the God who made you, knows you, and loves you.

You have searched me, Lord,
   and you know me.
You know when I sit and when I rise;
   you perceive my thoughts from afar.
You discern my going out and my lying down;
   you are familiar with all my ways.
Before a word is on my tongue
   you, Lord, know it completely.
You hem me in behind and before,
   and you lay your hand upon me.
Such knowledge is too wonderful for me,
   too lofty for me to attain.

Where can I go from your Spirit?
   Where can I flee from your presence?
If I go up to the heavens, you are there;
   if I make my bed in the depths, you are
      there.
If I rise on the wings of the dawn,
   if I settle on the far side of the sea,
even there your hand will guide me,
   your right hand will hold me fast.
If I say, "Surely the darkness will hide me
   and the light become night around me,"
even the darkness will not be dark to you;
   the night will shine like the day,
   for darkness is as light to you.

For you created my inmost being;
    you knit me together in my mother's womb.
I praise you because I am fearfully and wonder-
      fully made;
    your works are wonderful,
    I know that full well.
My frame was not hidden from you
    when I was made in the secret place,
    when I was woven together in the depths of
      the earth.
Your eyes saw my unformed body;
    all the days ordained for me were written in
      your book
    before one of them came to be.
How precious to me are your thoughts, God!
    How vast is the sum of them!
Were I to count them,
    they would outnumber the grains of sand—
    when I awake, I am still with you.[14]

---

[14] Psalm 139:1–18 NIV

Reflection Questions

1. When dealing with destructive, habitual
    thoughts and behaviors, Christians tend
    to focus on the first two enemies listed in
    this chapter: the sin nature and Satan.
    Why do you think we are reluctant to focus
    on story as a contributing factor?

2. Think for a moment about a fearful, self-
    ish, angry, or prideful tendency that lurks
    in your heart and rears its ugly head from
    time to time. Write it down. Have you felt
    guilt over it, repeatedly confessed it to
    God, and asked him to remove it? Can you
    peel back the layers of motivation to a part
    of your story that might have set the stage
    for this thought or action?

3. Write down the wound you carry from
    your story that has had the biggest effect
    on the story you are currently writing. Now
    write a prayer, asking God to apply his
    healing salve to that wound so that you
    can continue writing through the lens of
    his perfect love.

5

THE STORY OF THE LOVE YOU RESPONDED TO

The question is not "do you love your children?" It's "do they feel loved?"

– Gary Chapman[1]

Expressing loving support is of paramount importance within the family structure . . . Without the balance of love and limits, children are robbed of the wholeness God intended them to have.

– Gary Smalley[2]

Before we turn back the clock and examine our story through the lens of parental love, I feel it is necessary to answer the skeptic. Why are we going back and evaluating how our parents loved us? Didn't we lay the foundation in chapter one that our identity cannot be conferred upon us by anyone but God, our creator? Yes, it is true that even the people who raised us cannot give us our true

---

[1] Gary Chapman, "Fill Up the Lovetank in Your Marriage - An Interview With Dr. Gary Chapman," interview by Leh Meriwether & Todd Orston, Divorce Team Radio Podcast, Episode 55, Posted on February 16, 2020, https://mtlawoffice.com/podcast/the-five-love-languages-an-interview.

[2] Gary Smalley, *The Key To Your Child's Heart* (Dallas: Word Press, 1992), 62.

identity. However, the way they raised us might make it easier or harder for us to trust our God-given identity.

Parents have the crucial responsibility of raising children who understand God loves them. This understanding is imparted not just through bringing them to Sunday School and teaching them John 3:16. Church attendance and Scripture memory are good and important for a child's theological training, but far more important than imparting knowledge is imparting love. Parents are the proxy for God, especially during the earliest years of a child's development. The person who they trust most is not God; it is Mom and Dad. If Mom and Dad communicate through word and deed that they love their child, they are, in essence, modeling God's love for that child. As the child grows through adolescence into young adulthood, he will have an easier time believing God loves him if his parents have loved him. This lays the foundation for a healthy self-concept.

The tie between parents' love and God's love is so strong that young children often cannot tell them apart. Many of us carry a skewed view of God's love with us into adulthood because of how our parents loved us. If, for example, you were raised by parents who had high performance expectations and showed major disappointment when you failed, you will most likely believe God's love is conditional based on your performance.[3] On the flip side, if you were raised by permissive, indulgent parents who had few behavioral expectations, you will most likely struggle to see God's discipline as love.[4]

---

[3] Titus 3:5
[4] Hebrews 12:6

It is impossible to escape childhood without some identity lies to undo, no matter how Christ-like your parents were. Our identity is what we believe to be true about ourselves, and our true identity is found in who God believes us to be. Therefore, we must take the time to untangle the aspects of our parents' love that aligned with God's love from those aspects that contradicted it.

Blame and Guilt

We have all been loved imperfectly by our parents because none of us were raised by Jesus. As you read the following stories, resist the temptation to assign blame and hold grudges. Looking back to the imperfect ways you were loved is not a blame game! The last thing I want you to do is to cast blame on your parents for your dysfunction or use your past as an excuse for your current destructive behavior. Looking back is step one of your journey toward true change, joy, and freedom. Please don't stop after step one. There are many more steps to come.

Another tendency we have is to pile on guilt and shame when confronted by our own weakness. If you are a parent, reading this chapter might be a painful reminder of the ways you have contributed to your children's identity lies. I'd like you to pray this prayer before you begin:

> God, I know I wasn't the perfect parent to my children. There are things I said and did that I can never go back and undo. Help me to not dwell on the past, which I can't change, but on my current and future actions, which I can change. By your grace, help me to love my

children better tomorrow, all the while entrusting their hearts to their perfect Heavenly Father.

As a mother to four children, I've been humbled by the impossible task I've been given. I have a boatload more grace for my parents in my forties than I did in my twenties, especially when I see they had their own identity hurdles to overcome.

The point of going back to your story isn't to assign blame or to heap up guilt but to understand why we act or think in certain ways. As painful as it might be to look back, the words, sentences, and paragraphs of the story that was written for you by your parents have to be examined first before you can allow God to overlay them with truth.

Rewind and Unwind

This undoing is not an easy task. Our responses to identity lies can be deeply ingrained and involuntary. As you read the next chapter, think about your recurring thought patterns, your reflexive attitudes and actions, and your most natural and immediate responses. Is there an identity lie you are believing that is the origin of those decisions or actions? Turn back the pages of your story and see if you can find the source of that lie. Did it come from the imperfect love of a parent?

The following true stories[5] are just a sampling of the imperfect ways in which parents love their children. Resist the temptation to dismiss them because they don't align with your story. You might have an

---

[5] The stories you will read in this chapter are true, but the names and details have been changed to ensure anonymity.

identity lie that comes from a parenting style not listed. You might identify with a parenting style listed, but your outcome is a completely different identity lie. The point is not to put people into neat categories but to give some examples of lies that are sown in childhood and carried into adulthood. It is up to you to plumb the depths of your own story to unearth the sources of your unique identity lies.

Abandonment

When Katie was only a few months old, her mother left her in the care of her great aunt so she could pursue a singing career. Katie pretended not to feel the sting of this abandonment, even when she didn't receive birthday cards or phone calls. As a way to cope with her pain, she told herself she was lucky to have the loving support of her great aunt. Deep down, however, she felt unloved and unlovable, especially because her mom hadn't sent her brother and sister away, only her. At fourteen, she fell in with a bad crowd and started doing drugs. At sixteen, she met a boy who she thought was the love of her life. He was older, had a good job, and, with the absence of a father figure in her life, she was desperate for someone to love and take care of her. She was immediately drawn by his charisma and his smooth-talking charm, but when she was eighteen, soon after they were married, he became abusive and controlling. Slowly, he narrowed her world by not allowing her to go to school, to work, to a doctor, or to church.

Even though she became a Christian in her teens, Katie couldn't shake her earliest identity lie of not being loveable enough to be wanted by her mom. When she finally gathered the courage to leave her abusive husband, she fell into a cult Christian group led by an abusive man. She devoted twenty years of her life to that group before her eyes were finally opened to the spiritual abuse when the leader molested her own daughter.

After twice being the victim of abusive men, she spent the last several years figuring out why she is drawn by their strength and charm. She is learning to entrust her heart to her new husband, who is the opposite of her first one. Now, in her fifties, she is finally starting to believe she is cherished by God. This bedrock truth has begun to change not only how she sees herself but also how she relates to other people.

The Identity Lie

Adults whose parents gave them up to be raised by someone else often believe the identity lie "I am unwanted or unlovable." Many subconsciously believe they must have done something to cause their parents to abandon them.

The Behavior Clues

The lie that stems from this type of story negatively impacts an individual's self-worth and, if it is not corrected with God's truth, could lead them to either victimize or become a victim. Counselor to adoptees Nancy Verrier writes, "Despite the continuity of relationship which adoption provides, many adopted children experience themselves as unwanted, are unable to trust the permanency of the adoptive relationship and often demonstrate emotional disturbances and behavioral problems."[6] In Katie's case, even though she was blessed by the loving presence of her great aunt, she couldn't shake the belief that she was unwanted by her mom. This led her to abuse her body with drugs and endure the abuse of two men.

The identity lies that accompany abandonment can also manifest in relationships.

> Adult adoptees whom I have seen in treatment, most of whom did not act out in childhood, speak of having a sense that the baby they were "died," and that the one that they became was going to have to be different, to be better, so that he would not be abandoned again. Many became "people pleasers," constantly seeking approval . . . They could never truly bond with anyone because they were not being themselves. They related an inability to show how they felt about things, especially negative feelings.[7]

But as God is prone to do, he causes beauty to emerge from the most unlikely places.[8] Adults who were abandoned as children are often committed to rescuing children from abandonment. Some of the most compassionate, committed foster and adoptive parents have come from homes where they were themselves abandoned. Katie went back to school to earn her teaching degree and is now teaching in a low-income public school.

---

[6] Nancy Verrier, "Adoption: The Primal Wound: Effects of Separation from the Birthmother on Adopted Children," 2, PDF, https://adopta.hr/images/pdf/the_primal_wound.pdf.

[7] Nancy Verrier, "Adoption: The Primal Wound," 11.

[8] Isaiah 61:3

Self-Focused Parenting

Tammy and Mike have been happily married for twenty-six years and have raised two smart, beautiful daughters. As her girls were growing up, Tammy tried hard to give them everything they needed physically, emotionally, and spiritually. Her guiding principle in parenting, however, was to be the exact opposite of her mother.

Tammy's mom and dad divorced when she was eight, leaving her and her sister to be raised almost solely by her mom. Growing up, she never remembers an extended period of time when her mom was sober. Her mother was a functioning alcoholic who managed to hold down a steady job and provide for her girls but was drunk every night and all weekend long. Even though the topic of her mom's drinking was never discussed, she remembers going to the fridge and measuring her mom's wine intake with a Sharpie on the bottles. She also remembers missed opportunities to participate in events because her mom was asleep and couldn't drive.

Tammy and her sister were forced to be responsible because of their mother's negligence, which left Tammy with the identity statement "I am on my own." This sense of having no one to depend on was physical—she remembers feeling a pit in her stomach every time she saw her mom's car in the driveway when she got home from school. It was also emotional. Most of the time she saw vulnerability as too risky, even with her closest friends. After they had dated a month or two, Mike went out on a limb and expressed his feelings for Tammy by saying, "I love you." There was a long awkward silence, and Mike, feeling embarrassed, fished for a reply. All she could say was, "I don't feel anything. I don't think I'm capable of feeling love."

When it came to her faith, Tammy believed God loved her from a distance, but she could not comprehend how God could care intimately about her. She followed rules because they made sense and also because it was a comfortable way of expressing her love for God, but she never had any expectation of a close relationship with him. She didn't expect anything from him, really.

It has only been in recent years, with help from a counselor, that Tammy has been able to see vulnerability and dependence in a relationship as positive. She is learning to open up and share her emotional needs with close friends and family without fear.

The Identity Lie

Because of the story that was written for them, adults raised by parents who prioritized themselves above their children will believe Tammy's identity lie of "I am on my own" or perhaps "I am too needy." These are conditioned responses set in motion by the many instances where, as children, they were either criticized when they shared a need or felt they couldn't even have needs, since their parents were focused mainly on meeting their own needs.

The Behavior Clues

Because they never felt that they could rely on their parents, some people raised in these homes will bottle up their emotional needs for years, which can sadly lead to substance abuse or mental health issues. They have difficulty setting appropriate boundaries in relationships, which leads either to seething resentment or frequent, angry flare-ups. Some of those scarred by their parents' selfishness are deeply distrusting of anyone who tries to get too close. They are skeptical of expressions of affection, especially if they mirror the expressions used by a parent to compensate for periods of self-indulgent neglect. They use cynicism as a self-protection mechanism and often push away the people who are closest to them. Others, like Tammy, see vulnerability in relationships as a threat to their sense of independence and control.

Dr. Janet Woititz published the widely-known book *Adult Children of Alcoholics* in 1983. In it, she outlined thirteen characteristics of adult children of alcoholic parents. She then applied these same characteristics to those who grew up in households where other compulsive behaviors are present, such as gambling, drug abuse, or overeating. Not every adult child of an addict displays every characteristic, but some of the more common markers are:

- Fear of losing control
- Fear of emotions or feelings
- Avoiding conflict
- Harsh self-criticism and low self-esteem
- Difficulties with intimacy[9]

Again, not everything is bad news. A positive attribute frequently seen in children who grew up with self-centered parents is an exceptional work ethic and intrinsic motivation. They do not expect handouts,

---

[9] Janet G. Woititz, *Adult Children of Alcoholics: Expanded Edition* (Deerfield Beach: Health Communications, Inc., 1983), Introduction, Kindle Edition.

and they will dig in and work hard without needing external prodding. Another positive outcome is deep loyalty and fierce devotion. They may only let a few people into their circle of trust, but once they do, they will never walk away. Tammy says she feels this way about her own children, sometimes going overboard to meet their needs in order to spare them the neglect she felt as a child.

Authoritarian Parenting

Aaron is a strong, confident man with a successful business, an immaculate house, a beautiful wife, and two adorable young children. He cares a lot about his health, as evidenced by his muscle-bound forearms and perpetual water bottle sipping. Aaron admits that his life now is enviable by all accounts, but it hasn't always been this way.

When I asked Aaron to describe his dad's parenting in one word, he said "oppressive." With his dad, there was no differentiating between minor and major offenses. Everything was major. He and his siblings were made to feel they were a nuisance to their dad, barely tolerated, and chastised for every childish mistake. He told me one story to illustrate the pettiness of his dad's grievances and controlling nature. When he was twelve, he was helping his dad install lights in their basement. Standing on a ladder, holding up the light fixture for several minutes while his dad screwed it in, he made a reflexive grunting noise in response to his tired shoulder muscles. His dad took this to mean he was complaining about the hard work and spent the next several minutes berating him for his weakness.

Living under the constant displeasure of his authoritarian father, Aaron took on the identity of "small" or "fragile." He did everything he could to gain the approval of adults and peers. In high school, he became a class clown, but describes himself as cowardly, never standing up for himself, and always going along with the crowd. Perhaps to allay his self-doubt and his identity of smallness, Aaron joined the army and spent two-and-a-half years in the military, including one combat tour in Kuwait. But even being around tough men and rising to difficult physical and mental challenges couldn't assuage the timidity that he felt within himself. When he got out of the army, he decided that if he couldn't feel strong, he would make himself strong. He essentially played the part until he felt it, and his method worked in every relationship but one.

His relationship with his father finally came to a head after years of working in the family business. Following several screaming matches with his father over lack of confidence and trust in Aaron as a competent employee, he decided to quit the business and sever ties with his dad. One morning, as he cried out to God about the unfairness of the situation, God impressed upon him that he needed to submit—to be vulnerable with his dad about his wounds and to trust God to be the kind Father that his earthly father was not. In the bravest act of his life, he met his dad for breakfast, told him he did not want to quit the business or give up on the relationship, but he could not take the berating any longer. For the first time ever, he expressed how much his father had crushed his spirit over the years with his harshness. In that moment, God melted his father's heart toward him.

Aaron still has a hard time believing that God loves him unconditionally, but he has come to appreciate—with all his strengths and weaknesses—who God made him to be.

The Identity Lie

Adults whose stories have been written by controlling or authoritarian parents will believe the identity lie "I am fragile and vulnerable," or "I am weak and powerless."

The Behavior Clues

Authoritarian parenting is defined as being high in demands and low in responsiveness.[10] Adults raised in these homes often react in two distinct ways. One reaction is to do everything in your power to stop feeling vulnerable, which usually results in outward shows of strength without curing the fragility inside. Many of the biggest bullies have had hyper-controlling parents. Another reaction is to be drawn to strong people who will protect you or make you feel stronger somehow. At best, the power dynamic of these relationships is skewed and unhealthy. At worst, it can lead to abuse.

In Aaron's case, he made a conscious decision to overcome his "smallness" by becoming physically "big" and by learning to stand up for himself. Rather than using that strength to make others feel small, he is using it to stand up for people who can't stand up for themselves. Among other causes, he heavily

---

[10] Kendra Cherry, "Eight Characteristics of Authoritarian Parenting: The Effects of Authoritarian Parenting on Children," *Very Well Mind*, May 5, 2019, https://www.verywellmind.com/what-is-authoritarian-parenting-2794955.

supports a local ministry to rescue and protect women trapped in sex trafficking.

Codependent Parenting

Jenna's mom was convinced her happiness depended on the love she received from her children. The sad truth was, however, that Jenna could never do enough to make her mom feel loved. Her mother had such a bottomless pit of her own that, no matter how much her children tried to love her, she was never filled.

Her mother's neediness—what psychologists have now defined as codependence[11]—was expressed in jealous fits over Jenna's relationship with her dad, days of silent treatment for perceived mistreatment, and harsh critique of a dance recital at age five that caused Jenna to quit ballet. Her mother's emotional manipulation continued into adulthood, with the expectation that Jenna put her mother's needs above even her own husband and children. Sadly, she died with only Jenna by her side, having pushed away every other loved one in her life with her demands.

Because she always felt she was responsible for her mother's happiness, Jenna developed a "caretaker" identity, convinced the only way people would like her is if she served them and tried to meet their every need. In elementary school, she was the teacher's pet, volunteering for every minor chore to please her teachers. In high school, she was voted

---

[11] Lana Blackmoor, "Eight Signs You May Have a Codependent Parent," *We Have Kids*, December 16, 2016, https://wehavekids.com/family-relationships/8-Signs-You-May-Have-a-Codependent-Parent.

biggest flirt for her constant attempts to get positive affirmation from boys. She became a Christian as a teenager, but the people-pleasing and feelings of having to earn love from God and others did not change until much later in her life. Her choices in men were the natural product of her insecure caretaker identity, including an emotionally and physically abusive first husband and a verbally and emotionally abusive second husband.

The turning point for Jenna's identity was when she went through an intense women's Bible study group at her church, where she was forced to go back through her past and uncover the lies she believed about her identity. She describes this period as "laying down idols" and allowing God to fill the holes that were left. Today, she is a changed woman. She still serves people, but now she does so out of an overflow of Christ's love. She is confident in who God has made her to be, and she no longer needs people's affirmation to make her feel loved. Her children and husband have noticed this difference and are beginning to respect and love this new confident version of herself.

The Identity Lie

Adults raised by codependent, needy parents will believe the lie "I am responsible for the happiness of the people around me." This is because they were heavily relied on as a child to meet the emotional needs of their parents.

The Behavior Clues

Let's start with the positive quality of people who believe this identity lie. They make excellent caregivers. They are quick to set aside their desires and needs and are highly attuned to the needs of the people around them.

However, their caregiving comes more out of a need to be accepted than from an abundant overflow of love. If they don't replace this identity lie of being responsible for people's happiness with God's truth, they will only feel good about themselves when the people they care for are happy. This will lead to them blaming themselves when people are unhappy or behave badly. They will choose spouses and friends who they can take care of and will often be disappointed by the love they receive in return. Psychologist Kathy Hardie-Williams also warns children of codependent parents that they may perpetuate the cycle by parenting their own children in similar ways.[12]

Withdrawn Parenting

Mark is a smart, funny, creative, and successful husband and father. When I asked him how he sees himself, however, the first word that came to his mind was "uninteresting." I was curious. Why did he see himself this way when I and many others see him as anything but boring?

Mark is the youngest of three children, raised by an alcoholic mom and a disconnected father. He describes his mom as being mainly "clueless," meaning she tried to be a good mom but had no tools. He described his father, however, as unavailable, distant, and completely hands-off. He was a school teacher,

---

[12] Kathy Hardie-Williams, "Codependency and Parenting: Breaking the Cycle in Your Family," *Good Therapy*, November 17, 2015, http://www.goodtherapy.org/blog/codependency-and-parenting-break-the-cycle-1117155.

which you would think would make him great with kids and available all summer long, but it was just the opposite. When his dad wasn't at school, he was holed up in his office grading papers. On Saturdays, he worked a second job and during summers he worked on continuing his education. Mark made attempts to build a relationship with his dad by faking interest in the science-y things his dad was into, but his dad made no attempts to get to know him. In high school (the same school where his dad taught), one of his teachers stopped him at lunch and said, "I was telling your dad the other day how funny you were, and he said, 'Really? Mark's funny?' Doesn't your dad know you are funny?" When he wasn't surprised by his dad's reaction, the teacher remarked how sad that was. It was the first time it occurred to Mark that maybe his dad's disinterest was abnormal.

Naturally, Mark has overlaid his dad's disinterest onto God, finding it almost impossible to believe God would notice him unless he did something extraordinary. When things are going well, he feels he doesn't deserve God's blessing. When life is difficult, he figures it is due to some failure on his part, again reinforcing the narrative that he is not interesting enough to be on God's radar.

In his marriage, he sometimes feels like he cannot get enough affirmation from his wife, and he admits he half expects her to get tired of him someday and leave.

With his kids however, he is making every effort to make sure they know he cares deeply about their lives. He constantly encourages them in their pursuits, making time to listen to them and offer them wisdom. He rejects the notion that more "stuff" will make them happy (something his parents both believed), and instead he offers them the quality time children crave. Mark's confidence in his parenting is building day by day as he works hard to build up the self-esteem of his kids.

The Identity Lie

If you were raised by a parent who loved you from afar, providing for your physical needs but leaving gaping wounds because of their emotional distance, you probably believe some version of Mark's identity lie "I am uninteresting." Maybe you feel inconsequential or invisible.

The Behavioral Clues

Seeing yourself as inconsequential can show up in different ways, depending on your personality. If you are more outgoing and assertive, you may become an attention hog, perpetually seeking reassurance that you really are interesting. If you are more reserved, like Mark, you will probably blend into the wallpaper, waiting for someone to notice you. In her article on emotionally distant parenting, child trauma specialist Támara Hill writes, "Having an emotionally unavailable parent or guardian can lead to a lifelong journey of unstable or failed relationships, emotional neediness, empty voids, identity confusion, poor attachment to others, low self-esteem and self-efficacy (the feeling of mastery), etc."[13]

---

[13] Tamara Hill, "Seven Consequences of Having an Emotionally Detached Parent," *PsychCentral*, Last Updated January 22, 2018, https://blogs.psychcentral.com/caregivers/2016/03/7-consequences-of-having-an-emotionally-detached-parent/.

One positive outcome from having grown up with emotionally distant parents is you probably have a passion for helping others discover and nurture their unique talents and interests. Some of the strategies you developed for coping with distant parents could be positive as well. Mark attributes his humor and creativity to coping with his lonely home environment.

Indulgent Parenting

Lana grew up in a stable home with loving, supportive parents who doted on their two daughters. Her dad worked hard to provide a comfortable middle-class life for his girls, and her mom stayed home. They lived in a white-collar suburb and the girls attended top rated public schools and private colleges. Her parents praised her effusively and never missed a track meet or piano recital. If she needed something, she knew she could ask, and her parents would deliver.

What identity issues could possibly come from such a wonderful home, you might ask? Because Lana was overly praised as a child, she saw herself as not valued unless her accomplishments were noticed. She discovered as an adult that she was a praise-addict. In her marriage, she has at times felt unloved by her husband because he doesn't dole out the affirmation she was accustomed to receiving. If he doesn't compliment her for some task she performs, she will sometimes get on the phone with her mother, who will reliably give her the praise boost she craves. She admits she avoids failure at almost all costs, preferring instead to not try at all than to try and fail.

In her relationship with God, she finds it difficult to rest in his grace and acceptance without needing to earn his affirmation. One of the most confusing and disillusioning times in her faith came after she had poured her heart and soul into helping a friend, even taking her in for several weeks, only to have her turn on Lana with accusations and slander. Lana's pain in receiving this criticism was compounded by the intense pleasure of God she had felt during the season of sacrificing and caring for her friend. How could doing something she felt would please God end with the exact opposite of praise and affirmation? What good had come from her efforts? She admits she has been reticent to minister in this way again after being hurt so badly.

As Lana grows and matures, she needs people's affirmation less and less. She is learning to trust that God loves her without performance strings attached. As she parents her own children, her number one goal is to model and foster a relationship with God, not just a list of duties to check off. She is parenting her own children with less indulgence than she received and wants to instill in them the values of resilience and hard work.

The Identity Lie

There are many reasons parents indulge their children. Some are reacting to harsh, strict parents who damaged their self-esteem with never-ending critique. Some are reacting to growing up in extreme poverty, vowing to give their children everything they did not have. Some are following the child-rearing method of the day, believing that parents can instill confidence in their children by praising them for every little thing.

Whatever causes parents to equate love with indulgence, the outcome is a group of adults like Lana who believe the identity lie "I am not valuable unless I am being affirmed." Some might grow up believing "I am better than everyone else" because they were artificially pumped up with their parents' praise.

The Behavior Clues

Depending on how indulgent the parents were, the behavior clues can vary in severity from craving affirmation like Lana, to being entitled, arrogant, and incapable of empathy. Some crumble when criticized, giving up after trying once or twice, and blame failure on outside forces. Success to the indulged child is measured by people's attention and affirmation, and failure is being unnoticed or forgotten.

The first chapter of Po Bronson and Ashley Merryman's book *Nurture Shock* is called "The Inverse Power of Praise." In it, the authors chronicle the findings of researcher Dr. Carol Dweck, who studied the effect of praise on students in twenty New York schools for ten years. Her findings revealed that praising kids for their innate characteristics instead of their effort had the opposite intended effect: those children whose innate characteristics were praised later gave up quickly, did not even try difficult challenges, and had a lower self-esteem when they failed. Dweck says, "When we praise children for their intelligence, we tell them that this is the name of the game: look smart, don't risk making mistakes . . . Excessive praise also distorts children's motivation; they begin doing things merely to hear the praise, losing sight of intrinsic enjoyment."[14] Other analysis of research by Reed College and Stanford professors concluded that "Praised students become risk-averse and lack perceived autonomy."[15]

On the positive side, people who need affirmation tend to be generous with their affirmation of others. Often, if the indulgence they received was material, they will be quick to give generously without considering the work required to earn that gift.

Parenting with Conditional Love

Many mornings, Amanda wakes up in a panic: heart racing, palms sweating, gasping for breath. It takes several minutes for cognition to kick in and remind her she has nothing to fear, and most days she is able to shake off the cloud. Some days, however, the darkness remains.

Amanda was raised by a mother who she describes as authoritarian and distant, with narcissistic tendencies, while also possessing the ability to be gregarious and affable. Most of the people who knew her mother would be surprised to know her children had to tread carefully around her. Her mom wasn't the loud, angry type, but her disapproval was keenly felt in passive aggressive behavior, mood swings, and withdrawal. Amanda's overwhelming emotion throughout her childhood was fear—fear of doing something to lose her mom's favor and fear of not being able to do enough to earn it back. However, the "favor" granted by her mother did not take the form

---

[14] Po Bronson and Ashley Merryman, *Nurture Shock: New Thinking About Children* (New York: Twelve, 2009), 14, 20–21.
[15] Bronson and Merrymen, *Nurture Shock*, 21.

of warmth and affection but of basic safety and normalcy. A good day was one in which her mom seemed happy and satisfied by the good behavior of her children.

A childhood scarred by the conditional love of her mother left Amanda with the identity lies "I am unlovable" and "I am inadequate." She remembers being desperate for close friends so she could feel safe. In high school and college, she tried to satiate her fears with physical love from men, but every relationship only served to reinforce her belief that she was unlovable and inadequate. These twin lies fueled her over-achieving academic career, driving her to earn multiple advanced degrees. On the outside, she is smart, beautiful, poised, and compassionate. On the inside, however, she still believes that if people knew the real Amanda they would not accept and love her.

In recent years, with the help of a good Christian therapist, she has had breakthroughs, especially as it relates to her feelings of inadequacy. She no longer feels the desperate need to make safe friends, and she is much better at being able to brush off criticism. She is learning to take control of her thoughts, choosing to listen to the voice of truth rather than the instinctive lies that pervade her mind. Although she still has reservations, she is beginning to believe she is loved fully and completely by God.

The Identity Lie

As a result of the story that was written for them, adults raised by parents who loved them conditionally often believe the same identity lie as Amanda: "I am lovable only when I am performing well."

If you're a parent, you know how hard it is to maintain the balance of reassuring a child she is loved while at the same time conveying disapproval for bad behavior and reinforcement for good behavior. It is a tightrope all parents walk. The identity lie "I am only lovable when I perform well" is not necessarily sown by a few parental missteps but by regularly withholding love based on a child's performance. When children raised in conditional love fail, they feel not just the sting of disappointing their parents but also the pain of relational distance. Unless they replace this lie with the truth of God's unconditional love for them, they will be plagued by feelings of inadequacy their whole lives.

The Behavior Clues

If you were raised by a parent whose love was conditional, these feelings of inadequacy can manifest in different ways depending on how you think you're performing. If you are performing well, you feel good about yourself and you feel you deserve love from God and people. If you are not doing well, you feel terrible about yourself and you believe you deserve God's punishment or peoples' nasty treatment. You may have difficulty revealing weakness to others because you fear you will lose their love or admiration. As a result, you feel like an imposter, positing a successful persona to the world while hiding the real you, which you believe is not good enough for public consumption. These feelings can snowball into depression or anxiety, both of which cloud your mind from seeing any good in yourself and make it harder to uproot the identity lie.

This quote by family therapist Kathy Caprino is about people raised by narcissists, but it applies to anyone raised with conditional love. "Adult children of narcissists can live their entire lives (unless they get help to heal and overcome it) thinking they're not good enough and seeking validation and recognition at every turn, yet never feeling they get it. Often, children of narcissists are overly-sensitive, deeply insecure, unable to see themselves as good, worthy and lovable."[16]

Some positive behaviors can stem from this lie as well. The highest achievers in our world tend to come from homes where their love and acceptance depended on their performance. These are the responsible, task-oriented, self-disciplined, straight-A students who go on to have brilliant careers and make a lot of money. But if they never replace their identity lie with the truth of God's unconditional love, they will always be seeking external acceptance and validation.

Self Reflection

Maybe you recognize your parents' failures or even some of your own parenting missteps in some of these stories. Maybe you see some of your patterns of thought or behavior, and you've never considered they might stem from an identity lie. Take some time now, before moving on to the next chapter, to analyze your story.

---

[16] Kathy Caprino, "How Being Raised By A Narcissist Damages Your Life And Self-Esteem," *Forbes Magazine*, July 6, 2016, https://www.forbes.com/sites/kathycaprino/2016/07/09/how-being-raised-by-a-narcissist-damages-your-life-and-self-esteem/#3851d7762c67.

Reflection Questions

Start at the beginning and work forward, asking your-self the following questions:

1. "How would I describe the overall parent-ing style I was raised with?"

2. "Did the way my parents loved me contrib-ute to an identity lie I've been believing?"

3. "Because my parents were _____, I believe I am _____."

4. "This identity lie underpins the following repetitive thoughts or behaviors: _____."

Start in the present and work backwards, asking yourself these questions:

1. "What are some of my habitual thoughts, reactions, or motivations?"

2. "Do any of these point to an identity lie?"

3. "I do/say/think _____ be-cause I believe I am _____."

4. "Do I believe that identity lie because of the way my parents loved me?"

5. Journal your answers to these questions and, when you are ready, move on to the next chapter to receive the truths to com-bat the lies.

6

THE STORY OF THE FATHER'S PERFECT LOVE

Self-rejection is the greatest enemy of the spiritual life because it contradicts the sacred voice that calls us the "Beloved." Being the Beloved expresses the core truth of our existence.

– Henri Nouwen[1]

Trying to boost our self-esteem by trying to live up to our own standards or someone else's is a trap. It is not an answer.

– Tim Keller[2]

I hope you spent some time after reading the last chapter to write down some of the lies you believe about yourself. You may have only one or you may have many. You may not be fully convinced those beliefs you carry about yourself are actually lies. You may have worked through many of these lies already, but remnants still linger. As long as we live in these earthly bodies, we will not fully understand the mind of God and the way he sees us. "For now we

---

[1] Henri J.M. Nouwen, *Life of the Beloved: Spiritual Living in a Secular World* (New York: The Crossroad Publishing Company, 2002), Chapter 1, Being the Beloved, Kindle Edition.
[2] Timothy Keller, *The Freedom of Self Forgetfulness* (Chorley: 10 Publishing, 2012), Chapter 2, Kindle Edition.

see only a reflection as in a mirror; then we shall see face to face. Now I know in part; then I shall know fully, even as I am fully known."[3]

However, you do not have to wait until you see God face to face to begin replacing lies with truth. God desires for you to be free from the lies that bind you, and he has given you the tools you need to break those fetters. I hope that by the end of this chapter you will be able to sort out the truth from the lies and begin to believe that what God believes about you is true!

Self-Esteem

You may have noticed the identity lies you wrote down were mostly value statements: "I am unlovable." "I am weak." "I am exceptional." The aspect of our identity most affected by the love we received from our parents is our self-esteem. Although some have married these two ideas, identity and self-esteem are not synonyms. Identity encompasses every belief we hold to be true about ourselves, whether positive, negative, or neutral. Self-esteem is a value-term, meaning it can only be used for how favorably or unfavorably you assess yourself.

If you were doted on and indulged by your parents, you may have an artificially inflated self-esteem. If you were ignored, abused, or rejected by your parents, you may have a deflated self-esteem. A healthy self-esteem is one in which you have the ability to accurately assess your strengths and weaknesses, yet still possess the self-worth to carry yourself with confidence, dignity, and humility.

---

[3] 1 Corinthians 13:12–13

If identity is the psychological buzzword for today, self-esteem was the buzzword from the 1980s and 90s. Psychologists espoused the idea that a high self-esteem was critical to a person's success and happiness, and thus critical to the overall health of society. "Many, if not most, of the major problems plaguing society have roots in the low self-esteem of many of the people who make up society."[4]

Once this premise was established in our collective consciousness, we set about finding ways to boost the self-esteem of our employees, students, and children. Self-help books lined the shelves, employers hosted seminars, Oprah inundated stay-at-home moms, therapists changed their methodology, and PSAs indoctrinated children during Saturday morning cartoons. Teachers, parents, and coaches were taught to overly compliment kids, never criticize a child, give everyone a participation trophy, and eliminate rating systems and competition that would make some children feel bad.

Today's young adults are now reaping the consequences of this bad methodology. Many of the methods used to boost self-esteem actually had the opposite outcome, creating a generation of less confident kids who needed to be praised and affirmed continually to feel good about themselves. The focus now has turned to creating resilient, hard-working kids by allowing them to fail and learn from their mistakes. Clearly culture's way of going about gaining a high self-esteem was all wrong. But was the premise

---

[4] Andrew Mecca, Neil J. Smelser and John Vasconcellos, *The Social Importance of Self-Esteem* (Berkeley and Los Angeles: University of California Press, Ltd., 1989), 1.

also wrong? Would most of society's problems really disappear if we all had healthy self-esteem?

While the vast majority of culture was testing out its self-esteem theories, many Christians, in typical puritanical fashion, decried this focus on self-esteem as sinful pride. Sermons were preached and books were written to warn us that the very concept of self-esteem was anti-biblical. Those doing the warning focused heavily on the fact that this idea had its origins in secular psychology, and therefore could not be trusted. They decried liberal Christian leaders for "ransacking" and "twisting"[5] Scripture in order to supply weak biblical support for this dangerous idea.

Conscientious Christians who heeded these warnings and sat under years of shame-based teaching became convinced that true Christ-like humility was found in self-condemnation. In his beautiful book, *The Return of the Prodigal* Son, Henri Nouwen writes, "For a very long time I considered low self-esteem to be some kind of virtue. I had been warned so often against pride and conceit that I came to consider it a good thing to deprecate myself."[6]

Many of today's Christians are no better off than those who raised their children with secular self-esteem methods. In some cases, Christians are worse off. Where non-Christians may have landed in therapy due to an artificially inflated self-esteem, Christians landed there with bottomed-out self-esteem and, in some cases, self-loathing.

---

[5] Jay E. Adams, *The Biblical View of Self-Esteem, Self-Love, and Self-Image* (Eugene: Harvest House Publishers, 1986), Chapter 6, Kindle Edition.

[6] Henri J. M. Nouwen, *The Return of the Prodigal Son: A Story of Homecoming* (New York: Doubleday, 1994), 107.

What Bible teachers missed in all their efforts to contradict secular psychology was that self-esteem was not a new idea originating from Freud and Jung. Self-esteem is woven into the creation narrative in Genesis. The very idea of humans being lovingly and intricately designed in the image of God and stamped with his likeness is a sharp rebuke to those who teach we must not love ourselves. The fall of man did not remove the Imago Dei. Though we are now born with hearts that bend away from God, Jesus did not tell us to erase ourselves but rather to remember who we are: God's beloved image-bearers. When we think or act in ways contrary to the Imago Dei, we do not cease to be image-bearers any more than a child ceases to be a son or daughter when they displease their parents.

A healthy self-esteem is crucial not only to our view of ourselves in relation to God, but also to our ability to carry out our purpose of imitating, representing, and glorifying God. Jesus makes this assumption when he commands us to "love your neighbor *as yourself*."[7] If we applied the self-deprecation taught by many church leaders to this verse, we would not be loving our neighbors well at all.

In chapter three, we asserted that self-acceptance was the first step to achieve the freedom and confidence necessary to live out our created ideal. But how do we attain self-acceptance? It is not by turning a blind eye to our weaknesses, nor by pumping up our strengths. It is through a proper understanding of God's acceptance of us. It is through believing the same thing God believes about us. Peter Kreeft says,

---

[7] Matthew 22:39, emphasis added

If God loves me, I must love myself—not coddle myself but respect myself, not idolize myself but love myself as I love my neighbor. Otherwise, I call God a fool. If God calls me precious and I call myself junk, I am calling God a liar . . . Self-esteem is necessary for all psychological health, and there is no absolutely sure basis for self-esteem other than the assurance of God's love for me.[8]

As Tim Keller says in multiple sermons on this topic, you gain self-esteem when the person you esteem most esteems you.[9] Who is worthy of all esteem? God. Who esteems you more than any other? God. Nouwen articulates it this way:

As the Beloved of my heavenly Father, "I can walk in the valley of darkness: no evil would I fear." As the Beloved, I can "cure the sick, raise the dead, cleanse the lepers, cast out devils." Having "received without charge," I can "give without charge." As the Beloved, I can confront, console, admonish, and encourage without fear of rejection or need for affirmation. As the Beloved, I can suffer persecution without desire for revenge and receive praise without using it as proof of my goodness. As the Beloved, I can be tortured and killed without ever having to doubt that the love that is given to me is stronger than

---

[8] Peter Kreeft, *The God Who Loves You* (San Francisco: Ignatius Press, 2004), 200.

[9] Tim Keller, "Our Identity: The Christian Alternative to Late Modernity's Story," a sermon given at Wheaton College on November 11, 2015, YouTube video, https://www.youtube.com/watch?v=Ehw87PqTwKw.

death. As the Beloved, I am free to live and give life, free also to die while giving life.[10]

To abolish the identity lies that are tied to our self-esteem, we must allow God to "re-parent" us. Armed with the knowledge that we are esteemed by our heavenly Father, we will have no choice but to esteem ourselves.

The Perfect Love of a Father

Because we are unique humans who receive love in a variety of ways, I will do my best to present the truth of God's love in several different forms. I'll begin with my words, then King David's, then some of my favorite hymns and poems. Take your time reading this section. Pause and consider every descriptor and apply it like medicine to your heart.

God loves you perfectly, unconditionally, wholeheartedly, and consistently. His love is not based on his moods or your performance. His love is not needy and requires nothing in return. He will never withhold his love from you.

He is with you right now, and he promises he will never leave you or forsake you. He is with you on the mountain top and in the valley. His heart aches when you are hurting, he laughs with you when you have bursts of joy, he is angry when you are mistreated, he beams with pride when you succeed.

---

[10] Nouwen, *The Return*, 39.

He knows what you need and will relentlessly pursue your holiness, even if that means allowing you to endure hardship. He delights in you. He is crazy about you. He is a proud Papa. He is your biggest fan. To prove how much he loved you, he sent his son to die for you. His son, Jesus, The Good Shepherd not only selected you and named you, he also laid down his life for you. You were worth dying for. You.

Amazing Love

God's love is the single greatest thought known to man. David wrote these beautiful words under the inspiration of the Holy Spirit. Read this slowly, out loud if you choose, and allow yourself to feel the Father's love bleeding through the poet's pen.

O my soul, bless God.
From head to toe, I'll bless his holy name!
O my soul, bless God,
don't forget a single blessing!

He forgives your sins—every one.
He heals your diseases—every one.
He redeems you from hell—saves your life!
He crowns you with love and mercy—a paradise crown.
He wraps you in goodness—beauty eternal.
He renews your youth—you're always young
in his presence.

God is sheer mercy and grace;
not easily angered, he's rich in love.
He doesn't endlessly nag and scold,
nor hold grudges forever.

He doesn't treat us as our sins deserve,
  nor pay us back in full for our wrongs.
As high as heaven is over the earth,
  so strong is his love to those who fear him.
And as far as sunrise is from sunset,
  he has separated us from our sins.
As parents feel for their children,
  God feels for those who fear him.
He knows us inside and out,
  keeps in mind that we're made of mud.
Men and women don't live very long;
  like wildflowers they spring up and blossom,
But a storm snuffs them out just as quickly,
  leaving nothing to show they were here.
God's love, though, is ever and always,
  eternally present to all who fear him,
Making everything right for them and their chil-
      dren
  as they follow his Covenant ways
  and remember to do whatever he said.

Bless God, all creatures, wherever you are—
  everything and everyone made by God.

And you, O my soul, bless God![11]

If nothing has captured your attention yet, how about some old poetry? I love hymns because they beautifully express Scripture and sound theology. Here are some snippets of some of my favorite hymns that convey the amazing wonder of God's intimate love for us. I encourage you to look up the entire text of each hymn and read them aloud.

---

[11] Excerpts from Psalm 103 from *The Message*

Love Divine, all loves excelling, joy of heaven to
   earth come down.
Fix in us thy humble dwelling, all thy faithful
   mercies crown.
Jesus, thou art all compassion, pure, un-
   bounded love thou art.
Visit us with thy salvation, enter every trembling
   heart.[12]

O Love that will not let me go, I rest my weary
   soul in thee.
I give thee back the life I owe, that in thine ocean
   depths its flow
May richer, fuller be.[13]

O the deep, deep love of Jesus, vast unmeas-
   ured, boundless, free.
Rolling as a mighty ocean in its fullness over me.
Underneath me, all around me, is the current of
   thy love.

Leading onward, leading homeward, to that glorious rest above.[14]
What wondrous love is this, that caused the Lord
   of bliss, to bear the dreadful curse for my
   soul?[15]

---

[12] Charles Wesley, "Love Divine All Loves Excelling" (Public
Domain, 1747), Lyrics found at Hymnary.org, https://
hymnary.org/text/love_divine_all_love_excelling_joy_of_he.

[13] George Mathison, "O Love That Will Not Let Me Go" (Public
Domain, 1882), Lyrics found at Hymnary.org, https://
hymnary.org/text/o_love_that_wilt_not_let_me_go.

[14] Samuel Trevor Francis, "O the Deep, Deep Love of Jesus"
(Public Domain, 1875), Lyrics found at Hymnary.org, https://
hymnary.org/text/o_the_deep_deep_love_of_jesus#Author.

[15] Anonymous, "What Wondrous Love is This?" (Public
Domain, 1811), Lyrics found at Hymnary.org, https://
hymnary.org/text/what_wondrous_love_is_this_o_my_soul_o_m.

See from his head, his hands, his feet,
Sorrow and love flow mingled down.
Did e'er such love and sorrow meet,
Or thorns compose so rich a crown?[16]

Could we with ink the oceans fill, and were the
　　skies of parchment made
Were every stalk on earth a quill, and every man
　　a scribe by trade;
To write the love of God above would drain the
　　ocean dry.
Nor could the scroll contain the whole, though
　　stretched from sky to sky.[17]

O love of God, how strong and true!
Eternal, and yet ever new;
Uncomprehended and unbought,
Beyond all knowledge and all thought.[18]

Loved with everlasting love, led by grace that love
　　to know;
Spirit breathing from above, you have taught me
　　it is so.
O what full and perfect peace, joy and wonder all
　　divine!

---

[16] Isaac Watts, "When I Survey the Wondrous Cross" (Public Domain, 1707), Lyrics found at Hymnary.org, https://hymnary.org/text/when_i_survey_the_wondrous_cross_watts.

[17] Frederick M. Lehman, "The Love of God" (Public Domain, 1917), Lyrics found at Hymnary.org, https://hymnary.org/text/the_love_of_god_is_greater_far.

[18] Horatius Bonar, "O Love of God, How Strong and True" (Public Domain, 1861), Lyrics found at Hymnary.org, https://hymnary.org/text/o_love_of_god_how_strong_and_true.

In a love which cannot cease, I am his and he is
  mine.[19]

The Truth versus The Lie

In case you are still unsure if what you are believing
about yourself is true, here is a list of lies spelled out
in black and white, as well as Scriptural truths to
combat them:

- When you believe you are unlovable, you
  are believing a lie (Jeremiah 31:3)
- When you believe you have to be good in
  order to be accepted, you are believing a
  lie (Romans 15:7)
- When you believe you are merely being tolerated, but not cherished, you are
  believing a lie (1 John 3:1–2)
- When you believe you are insignificant,
  you are believing a lie (Matthew 6:25–26)
- When you believe you deserve to be mistreated, you are believing a lie (Matthew
  10:28–30)
- When you believe you are on your own in
  this world and can trust no one but yourself, you are believing a lie (Deuteronomy
  31:6)
- When you believe you have gone too far or
  messed up too big to ever deserve to be
  loved, you are believing a lie (Romans 8:1)

---

[19] Wade Robinson, "I am His and He is Mine" (Public Domain,
1890), Lyrics found at Hymnary.org, https://hymnary.org/text/
loved_with_everlasting_love.

- When you believe you are weak and fragile, you are believing a lie (Romans 8:31)
- When you believe the bad things that happen to you are proof you are not loved, you are believing a lie (Romans 8:35)

These lies may have been your first beliefs about your identity based on the way you were loved by flawed humans, but these do not in any way reflect the kind of love your heavenly Father has for you.

These identity lies might be deeply buried within us. They might *feel* true. But you must learn to discern a lie from the truth. It is vital to regularly ingest and digest the truth. Just as the shadowy monsters that seem real in the night shift into familiar objects when the sun rises, when you turn up the light of truth in your heart, the lie will fade away.

The Big "T" Truth-Source

The ultimate source of truth is, of course, the Word of God. There is a power in reading those divinely inspired words, studying their meaning, and applying them like ointment to your soul. It might be helpful for you to write out some of the verses from the references above to counteract the lies you tend to believe about yourself. You might want to find more Scripture with similar truth and write the verses on cards and meditate on them throughout the day.

However, because our hearts are clouded by our fallenness, we may not know what lies we are believing. Even more important than targeting specific lies with verses is routinely reading Scripture and listening to the Holy Spirit. Dietrich Bonhoeffer writes,

Daily, quiet reflection on the Word of God as it applies to me (even if only for a few minutes) becomes for me a point of crystallization for everything that gives interior and exterior order to my life. The first few moments of the new day are not the time for our own plans and worries, not even for our zeal to accomplish our own work, but for God's liberating grace, God's sanctifying presence.[20]

Small "t" Truth-Sources

The Bible should be your go-to resource in finding out what God believes to be true about you. But there are a variety of other sources God can use to reveal his truth to you.

We will talk more about this in the next chapter, but it is vitally important to your understanding of self to be in community with other believers. Often other people can see you more clearly than you can see yourself. I cannot count the number of times I have sought counsel from a trusted friend and they have been able to shine a light on motives or habits where I was self-deceived. My husband is particularly (and annoyingly) good at asking the "Why" questions that get to the heart of my issues and help me see where I still believe identity lies.

God can also use tough circumstances to show you your identity lies. Several years ago, my parents drove their Dodge Intrepid from Connecticut to Washington to gift us a second car, which we badly needed. I loved that car because while I drove it I could

---

[20] Deitrich Boenhoeffer, *Meditating on the Word* (Lanham: Rowman & Littlefield Publishers, Inc., 2000), 42.

temporarily forget I was a middle-aged mom of four (our other car is, predictably, a mini-van). I drove it into Seattle every Tuesday for my choir rehearsals and to the grocery store while my kids were in school. One day, my husband drove it to a staff meeting at church and scraped the underside badly on an over-sized speed bump in the parking lot. He didn't think much of it and kept going with his day. Soon after, we noticed it leaking oil in the driveway but still didn't connect it to the speed bump incident. After a few weeks of progressively worse oil leaking and buying quarts of replacement oil, we decided to take it to the shop. On the way to the mechanic, the car seized up and stalled. The engine was ruined. We had to get it towed back to our house and ended up selling it for parts.

My reaction to this fiasco surprised me. See, as much as I loved this car, what upset me most was not that I could no longer feel young and carefree driving a new-ish car that didn't fit my whole family. It wasn't the loss of the convenience of having a second car. Nor was it the money required to tow the dumb thing. It was the feeling that I had failed. I had squandered the gift my parents had sacrificed to give us. I was so ashamed, I think I waited a whole week before calling my dad to tell him the embarrassing news.[21]

It took a while to process my reaction, but what I ultimately learned was that I was believing the identity lie of "I am only valued when I am receiving affirmation." I assumed this screw-up would deeply disappoint my parents (which it didn't, by the way)

---

[21] The ironic ending to this story is that a few months later, we were gifted a 1993 Chevy Suburban. Bigger than our mini-van, but perfect for family camping trips.

and God. I truly believed God could only love and bless me when I was a faithful steward of the resources he entrusted to me. Now that I had squandered this blessing, I didn't deserve another chance. I was still operating under a merit-based system of punishment and reward.

The thing is, for many years I had cognitively understood the theological concept of God's grace and unconditional love. I had read plenty of Scripture and many good books on the subject. I had even taught other people that God's love was without strings attached. However, it wasn't until I had failed that I was able to see the ways I still did not see myself the way God saw me.

Remember the story of the Wemmicks from chapter three? This is what visiting Eli the Woodcarver looks like.[22] It is physically going to his workshop by practicing the disciplines of scripture reading, prayer, silence, and worship. It is also paying attention to the ways he is speaking to you through your everyday life. In my life, God has used sermons, friends, books, songs, circumstances, and even my favorite NPR podcasts to get my attention and help me see the truth about how he sees me.

The Head and the Heart

A few years ago, when I was going through a particularly difficult season in my faith, God gave me this prayer. It became a theme for that season of my life, and it is now my prayer for you. Take note of God's

---

[22] Max Lucado, *You are Special* (Wheaton: Crossway Publishing, 1997).

desire for you to internalize his love and move it from the head to the heart.

> I pray that you, being rooted and established in love, may have power, together with all the Lord's holy people, to grasp how wide and long and high and deep is the love of Christ, and to know this love that surpasses knowledge—that you may be filled to the measure of all the fullness of God.[23]

In my own words:

> I pray that you, having your soul-roots firmly and deeply grounded in Christ's love, may have the ability, along with all your brothers and sisters in Christ, to understand the infinite stretch of the love of Christ in all directions, and to personally and intimately experience this love—which is impossible to explain through reason—that you may be filled to the brim and overflowing with Love itself.

---

[23] Ephesians 3:17–19

Reflection Questions

1. God wants to re-parent you by replacing old identity lies with the truth of his never-failing love. Look back to your reflection answers at the end of chapter five. Fill in the blanks:

   "Because my parents were/did/said _____, I believed I am _____. God tells me I am _____. I choose to believe him."

   Find a verse or two that supports the above statement. Write it down in your journal, and place it on sticky notes in at least two other places that you will see every day.

2. Write a letter to your parent(s), naming the lie that was unintentionally sown by them into the foundation of your identity. Be specific, but gracious, remembering all the ways they loved you well, and the ways they fought their own identity lies. When you are finished, pray over it, and ask God to heal those wounds. Discard the letter.

3. Think back on the circumstances of your story. Where has God been trying to get your attention? How has he proven his love to you?

7

THE STORY OF YOUR TRIBES

To be no part of any body, is to be nothing.
– John Donne[1]

A deep sense of love and belonging is an irreducible need of all women, men, and children. We are biologically, cognitively, physically, and spiritually wired to love, to be loved, and to belong. When those needs are not met, we don't function as we were meant to. We break. We fall apart. We numb. We ache. We hurt others. We get sick.
– Brene Brown[2]

W e've discussed one part of your story that contributed to the formation of your identity: the parental love you received. Another crucial identity chapter from your life is the tribes you belonged to. Both the groups you were born into and the groups you choose have a tremendous impact on what you believe to be true about yourself. We will spend this chapter dealing with the ways our earliest tribal experiences might have damaged our definition of self. In chapter nine, we will discuss how

---

[1] John Donne, *Selected Letters* (New York: Taylor and Francis Group, 2002), Letter XXV, Kindle Edition.
[2] Brené Brown, *The Gifts of Imperfection: Let Go of Who You Think You're Supposed to Be and Embrace Who You Are* (Center City: Hazelden Publishing, 2010), Chapter 2, Kindle Edition.

God can heal the identity wounds left by our tribes and how we can participate in community in healthy ways by following the example of Christ.

Humans are tribal creatures. As soon as there were enough of us on earth, we started grouping up. We form groups around shared skin color, language, affinity, gender—you name it and we've made a group out of it. In the late 1970s, British social psychologist Henri Tajfel and John Turner developed the theory of social identity, which asserted that humans develop their sense of who they are based on the tribes they belong to. According to Tajfel and Turner, there are three natural steps to the formation of groups: *classification*, or categorizing people according to gender, ethnicity, economics, etc., *identification*, or determining the category of people you most relate to, and *comparison*, or making judgments on those outside your group.[3]

We find the first two steps in the Genesis account pre-fall. Remember Adam's first job? He was tasked with naming, or *classifying*, the animal kingdom.[4] Among all the animals, however, he didn't find any he could *identify* with, so God created woman to be his equal.[5] It was not long after the fall that we find *comparison* happening in the story of Cain and Abel.[6] Once sin entered the picture we started seeking our identity in tribes, creating us/them categories and then using those categories to make ourselves feel

---

[3] Saul McLeod, "Social Identity Theory," *Simply Psychology*, Updated 2019, https://www.simplypsychology.org/social-identity-theory.html.

[4] Genesis 2:19

[5] Genesis 2:20–23

[6] Genesis 4:1–9

superior to outsiders. In other words, sin turned healthy communities into exclusionary ones.

This tendency to draw group boundaries and assert our group's superiority begins at a very young age. The book *Nurture Shock* cites a study of preschoolers conducted by Dr. Rebecca Bigler. In the study she divided classes into three teams and gave them colored t-shirts to represent their teams. Even though the teacher never made mention of the groups and the kids all played and ate together, when asked which group was "best" or "nicest" or "fastest," they all said their color group was. The conclusion from this study, and many others like it, is that "kids are developmentally prone to in-group favoritism."[7]

This tendency to compare and exclude is where we find the source of most of our identity wounds when it comes to tribes. Let's talk about the ways our earliest tribes might have damaged our identity in lasting ways.

When we don't "fit in" to our assigned tribe

Most of our tribes are ones we choose (or are chosen for us by our parents), such as where to live, what school to attend, and which church to join. But some of our tribes were assigned to us by virtue of our physical traits. Gender and race are two obvious examples. Before I go into how we are wounded by our assigned tribes, I want to be very clear that in this chapter I'm dealing with the social aspects of gender and race, not the physical ones. God in his wisdom created humans to be distinct from each other when

---

[7] Po Bronson and Ashley Merryman, *Nurture Shock: New Thinking About Children* (New York: Twelve, 2009), 53.

it comes to reproductive anatomy and skin color. Contrary to what some might assert, gender and race are not purely social constructs. Scientific studies have shown differences between the male and female brain, and there is no denying empirical evidence of physical racial differences, no matter how a person feels on the inside. However, there is a very powerful social component to these physical groupings.

As a young girl, my girlfriends played with dolls and My Little Ponies. I preferred to be outside playing in the dirt or building with Legos. As a teenager, my girlfriends were into gossiping about boys, doing each other's hair and nails, shopping, or talking on the phone. I would pretend I liked those things to fit in, but truthfully I had more in common with my guy friends. This feeling of not fitting in with the girls was compounded by the expectation in my Christian circles that boys should lead and girls should follow. All throughout my childhood and adolescence, I was labeled "bossy" when I asserted too much leadership or shared too many opinions. This made me feel even more like an outsider to my female tribe. As I matured and my world enlarged, I learned that the tribal boundaries of womanhood were more expansive than I was led to believe. I learned that there are many different kinds of women, and that I didn't have to force myself to enjoy making crafts and doing hair when I would rather be watching football and discussing philosophy. I could belong to my tribe without losing my individuality. However, the wounds left on my psyche from years of feeling like I did not fit in have taken many years to heal.

My friend Jake has similar wounds from growing up within a narrow definition of masculinity. His dad was a Baptist pastor in a tribe that glorified a stereo-typical misogynistic masculinity. Jake tried hard to fit in, even taking hunter safety classes, though he never actually went hunting. He preferred reading a book beside a lake to fishing in one, and he never took to sports. He found embroidery soothing to his over-active mind. The women in the church thought this was sweet—the boys and men, not so much. His own father suggested his son might be gay because he en-joyed more feminine activities. Jake himself questioned his sexuality during his adolescent years, only because the box he was forced into was much too small. There was no room in that masculine tribe for a quiet, thoughtful, creative bookworm like him. Like me, once he was out of the home and could see many men who were similar to him in personality and gifting, he learned to be comfortable in his gender tribe. Still, there are lingering remnants of the young Jake who yearns for validation from his fellow men.

Over the past thirty years, the Christian over-em-phasis on gender roles and distinctions has damaged many of us by making us feel like we don't belong in our gender tribes. I wonder how many young people have gone so far as to step outside their assigned gen-der in response to the tight gender boxes we have created. There are myriad ways to reflect the image of God as males and females, and we should not go fur-ther than Scripture goes in our attempts to nail down definitions of masculinity and femininity. Perhaps you too have felt on the "outside" of your assigned gender tribe at some point in your life. Even if you don't struggle to fit in now, take a moment and con-sider the insecurity caused by feeling different and the identity lies that might have lingered.

The social aspect of race can also cause people to feel they don't fit in with their assigned tribe. The pain is particularly sharp with mixed race people who aren't White, Black, Asian, or Hispanic enough to fit in with any racial tribe. My friend Susan, who was born in the US to a Korean mother and American father, describes instances of feeling too Asian at school and too American at home. At school, she endured martial arts and rice paddy jokes and even once had rocks thrown at her. At home, her mother fretted that she was becoming too American and parented her strictly for fear of losing her Korean roots. For her master's degree in fine arts Susan decided to do her final acting solo show on the topic of race, in particular on her experience of being biracial in America. Here is a segment from her show.

> I was getting married in a few days. I was excited. Excited enough to go out for a drink with a couple friends and my husband-to-be, which I never do. I don't care for the cigarette haze that hovers in bars making my lungs ache, or the need to shout in order to talk with the person next to you. But today I wanted to celebrate with my friends in town. I let them convince me to order what is called a "fish bowl" which I believe is a concoction of all sorts of evil alcohols thrown into a goldfish bowl. Pop in a straw and you've got yourself a drink. At first, the warmth feels good, though the taste is strong, and I enjoy the sensation as I slip into a relaxed state. I rarely drink, and my tolerance is low, so the alcohol hit hard and fast. Before long, I needed some fresh air. I felt claustrophobic, and longed to get outside, away from the cigarette smoke. Away from

the noise. Once outside, I took a deep breath in, and enjoyed the night world around me. I heard male laughter directly behind me. I turned around to see a group of five tall men in letterman jackets. They started circling me and taunting me. "Hey why don't you go back to where you came from?" What did that mean? Back in the bar? Where was my fiancé? I didn't realize that he didn't follow me out. They continued closing in. "Go back to your own country." My own country? The alcohol made my brain slow. My thoughts lagged, but my heart raced. I didn't know how to respond. This was my country. This IS my country. This is my country. But the words refused to form. I started to cry. And they walked away, congratulating themselves on their wit. I turned toward the bar, desperate to see a friendly face. Nobody seemed to notice me. Five men harass a woman on a busy sidewalk and nobody bats an eyelash. And this is my country.

The wounds Susan received from these experiences of not fitting in have taken their toll on her self-confidence and her relationships. If you've ever felt like an outsider in your assigned racial tribe, you know how soul-crushing it can be. Of course, Susan and millions of minorities around the world also feel the sting of being excluded from a tribe *because* of their race. This pain of being outside a tribe you are unable to join is another way your identity is affected by your earliest unchosen tribes.

When we are excluded from a tribe

Some of our greatest identity wounds come from being on the outside of groups we were denied access to. Aside from race, class and socioeconomic tribes are also powerful identity markers, whether you grew up rich or poor. Tarrah grew up in a poor family where food was rationed, shoes and clothes worn past the stage with holes, and family vacations only dreamed of. To this day, even though she and her husband own a nice house, two cars, and can afford vacations, she admits she still has trouble shaking the "poor kid" identity. She's not alone. In a 2013 article, researchers concluded that "for the 25 percent of American children currently living in poverty, the effects of low socioeconomic status will persist long into adulthood, even if their financial situation improves."[8] Some of these effects are physical—they are more prone to chronic disease and even early death, for example— but many are mental, such as disorders and "learned helplessness" due to most circumstances being out of their control. The same article states, "These trends held regardless of adult income levels, indicating that the effects of early childhood poverty are long-lasting and not simply corrected by better financial security later in life." This poverty identity is most easily observed in wealthy people who grew up in poor families. They may hoard food and clothing, they may spend lavishly or hardly at all. No matter how it manifests, they can never quite break free of seeing themselves as not having enough.

---

[8] Matt Repka, "Enduring Damage: The Effects of Childhood Poverty on Adult Health," *Chicago Policy Review*, November 27, 2013, http://chicagopolicyreview.org/2013/11/27/enduring-damage-the-effects-of-childhood-poverty-on-adult-health/.

Similar to socioeconomics, education draws clear tribal boundary lines.[9] Children who grow up with fewer educational opportunities in primary and secondary schools typically stay on the same trajectory for post-high school education, opting to enter the workforce after high school, or attending a vocational or community college. No matter the root causes of the disparity in educational opportunities from one community to another (teacher quality, funding inequities, poverty, and racial segregation to name a few), education inequity is an inescapable fact of our modern reality. The result is tribalism, based on the educational opportunities (or lack thereof) afforded to our citizens, and the chasm is widening year by year.[10] Just like a wealthy person who grew up poor has a hard time shaking the "poor kid" identity, many people who were not afforded a high quality education feel perpetually inferior to their peers who have diplomas and degrees, no matter how brilliant or successful they become. They still feel they are on the outside of a tribe they were denied access to.

---

[9] Matt Vespa, "Guardian Reporter: There Are Two Americas, A 'Front Row And The Back Row' . . . And Yes–Trump Exposed It," *Town Hall*, April 18, 2017, https://townhall.com/tipsheet/mattvespa/2017/04/18/guardian-reporter-there-are-two-americas-a-front-row-and-the-back-rowand-yestrump-exposed-it-n2314566.

Photo journalist Chris Arnade's conclusion, after driving 100,000 miles across the country in 2016 and interviewing hundreds of average Americans, was that there are two Americas—the front seat and the back seat—and the difference between the two comes down to education.

[10] *Educating All God's Children: What Christians Can—and Should—Do to Improve Public Education for Low-income Kids* by Nicole Baker Fulgham is an excellent resource for anyone wanting to further study educational inequity in our country.

When we are in the exclusive tribe

We all know the sting of feeling like an outsider, whether it is not fitting into our assigned tribe or being excluded from a tribe we desire to join. But what about the identity effects of being in a highly exclusive tribe? What are the lingering effects of being the one who is doing the excluding?

The fundamentalist church I grew up in made personal morality and separation from the world their defining purpose. This meant abstaining from alcohol, pop and rock music, television, and movies. In their efforts to be distinct, parents sent their kids to Christian schools, girls and women wore skirts and dresses, and boys and men had short hair. We were taught God was most pleased with us when we held the strictest personal standards. We were told the outside world was an enemy to fear and fight against. We even separated from other Christians who didn't hold our standards of separation. Talk about us versus them! Fundamentalist Christians wrote the book on being exclusive.

I've had two lingering identity effects of growing up in that bubble. One is fear. To keep the tribal narrative alive, our leaders sowed in us a great amount of fear as to what would happen if we got too chummy with the world. We were warned that exposure to all forms of worldly entertainment would turn our hearts away from God and that secular education might even cause us to lose our faith. We feared the displeasure of the tribe and of God himself if we strayed from its rules, and we feared exposing any weakness because the risks of doing so were too great. In response to all that fear-talk I built an identity that was afraid to be anything but perfect. I spent years hiding, protecting, and even lying because I had an identity of perfection to uphold. If anything challenged that identity, it had to be stuffed away lest I lose the thing that made me, me.

The second lingering identity effect of growing up in an exclusionary tribe is pride. When your whole life you are told your tribe is better than the rest, that your group alone is practicing true religion, and that God is most pleased with your brand of Christianity, the natural result will be arrogance and pride. It was a shock for me to discover later in life that there were many godly Christians outside the walls of my tribe. It was also humbling to realize that my pride was more of an affront to God than their indulgence in things I was taught to abstain from. The longer I live, the more humbled I become by the realization that I am no better than anyone else, and I deserve no special favor from God because of my supposed righteousness. But that prideful "better-than" identity runs deep. It has reared its ugly head more times in my life than I would like to admit.

Fear and pride are probably the markers of just about everyone who grew up in an exclusionary tribe. If you grew up with financial privilege, popularity, or athletic ability, you might fear going without, losing your social status or physical strength, or being seen with the wrong people. You might even fear those who grew up on the other side of the tracks from you, stereotyping them as dangerous. Pride is an obvious byproduct of growing up in an exclusionary tribe because you believe you are innately special and not just circumstantially privileged.

Tribalism

Belonging is not a sinful human desire. Primal, powerful, and universal, yes, but not sinful. When this desire is unfulfilled, however, it is the source of our most tender wounds. The natural tendency for all of us who have been wounded by our tribes is to seek out belonging in another tribe. Over and over again, I have seen adults try to find healing from their first unchosen tribes by seeking out or forming new tribes where they can belong. Those who were shut out from the popular crowd work hard to buy a house in an affluent neighborhood and do all they can to make sure their children don't experience the same rejection they felt. Those who were hurt by their gender seek out others like themselves and form new, more tolerant tribes where they are accepted. Those who were hurt by their church seek out another church or find belonging in secular tribes. To some degree, this rebound is not harmful. It is, however, easy to sink your identity into your new tribe to the point that you either become exclusive, protective, or defensive.

Underneath all the individualistic ideology of our age, a tenacious tribalism is bubbling to the surface in today's fractured society. We see this in the social climate of the West as established cultures are suddenly inundated with immigrants and refugees. Their way of life (i.e., their tribe) is threatened by the presence of people in their communities who don't look, talk, think, eat, or pray like them. Some respond by making more room at the table, but many fearfully circle the wagons to maintain their tribal identity. The practice of polite political debate has been replaced by "identity politics" where we take every philosophical disagreement as a personal affront to our identity. News organizations capitalize on this tribalization by catering stories to their constituents. We, the news consumers, insulate more and more into our social media thought bubbles by interacting only with those who agree with us. Many Christians, rather than taking Christ and the Gospel into culture, have retreated and created exclusionary tribes of their own, which then must be defended against threats from the secularized world.

> Prior to the Enlightenment, according to Martyn Atkins of England's Cliff College, people said, "I belong, therefore I am." Under the Enlightenment's influence, people said "I think, therefore I am." Postmodern people now seem to be saying "I feel, therefore I am." We also observe the "retribalism" of much of the West - as peer groups, subcultures, and ethnic groups produce an "I belong, therefore I am" source of identity once again.[11]

Tribal identity has always been a reality, but the unrest of the modern world is threatening to undo our tribes, which has caused many of us to rise up to defend them. The defense of our tribes has exposed how fiercely dependent upon them we are for our identity. If they disappear, who will we be?

---

[11] George G. Hunter III, *The Celtic Way of Evangelism: How Christianity Can Reach the West . . . Again* (Nashville: Abingdon Press, 2000), 97. This book stresses our current culture's need to "belong before they will believe."

The Better Way

In my youth, I sought belonging like a drug, and more often than not I ended up disappointed. One of the most blessed gifts of aging has been the ability to let go of the need to belong. I am more able, like Maya Angelou says, "to be at home wherever I find myself."[12] Jesus is our example of how to engage in tribes without staking our identity on them.

Jesus unapologetically identified with his tribes. He was a good Jew who attended Synagogue and festivals and learned the Torah inside and out.[13] As the firstborn male in his family, he took his responsibility seriously, attending to his grieving mother even from the cross.[14] He celebrated at weddings[15] and mourned at funerals.[16] He felt the pang of rejection from the townspeople who knew him best.[17] You would think rejection would cause him to isolate himself from community, but even when he started his public ministry, he didn't do it alone. He chose twelve men to be his new tribe, and he suffered greatly when he was betrayed by one and deserted by almost all.[18]

Jesus did not walk this earth devoid of any tribal ties. However, unlike us, he was able to separate who he *was* from who he associated *with.* He never lost sight of his ultimate purpose, even when it

---

[12] Maya Angelou Quotes. (n.d.). BrainyQuote.com. Retrieved November 17, 2017, from
https://www.brainyquote.com/quotes/maya_angelou_384166.
[13] Luke 2:40–52
[14] John 19:26
[15] John 2:1–11
[16] John 11
[17] Matthew 13:53–58
[18] John 13:21

contradicted the Judaism he was raised in.[19] He could endure rejection by his family and community because his sense of belonging was not tied to this earth.[20] He was able to leave the familiar and cross cultural boundaries because his desire for inclusion trumped his desire for comfort.[21] He was at home wherever he found himself, whether with his family, the adoring crowds, his disciples, the religious elite, or the beggars. He was grounded in a firm belief in who he was, allowing him the freedom to be in a tribe without defining himself by it.

---

[19] John 2:13–16
[20] John 10:30
[21] Matthew 11:19, John 4:1–26

Reflection Questions

1. We will talk more about following Jesus on the path to true purpose, belonging, and comfort in the next chapter, but before we do, take a minute to list out all your tribes chronologically from the earliest to the present.

2. Next, go down the list and ask yourself if you are defined by any of them, even if you've tried not to be. If you're not sure, fill in the blanks to this statement: "Because I was/am a part of the _____ tribe, I believe I am _____."

3. Are there any tribes you are still trying desperately to belong to? Are there any wounds from being rejected by a tribe? Do you feel superior to other tribes because of your tribal allegiances? If you lost your tribe for one reason or another, would you feel you had lost your sense of self?

8

THE STORY OF YOUR
TRUE TRIBES

Both the one who makes people holy and those who
are made holy are of the same family. So Jesus is
not ashamed to call them brothers and sisters.
– Hebrews 2:11

That day, all the Sneetches forgot about stars,
And whether they had one, or not, upon thars.
– Dr. Seuss[1]

I n the previous chapter, we ended with a brief
look at how Jesus engaged with tribes while he
was in human form. In this chapter, we will examine *how* he was able to do that, and we will see if
we can learn from his example.

Primary versus Secondary

The reason Jesus could engage with his tribes without tethering his identity to them is because he
understood the difference between primary and secondary tribes. Primary tribes are the true source of
purpose and belonging. They provide identity.

---

[1] Dr. Seuss, *Sneetches and Other Stories* (New York: Random
House, 1989), 24.

Secondary tribes may offer a measure of these things, but you will be misled and disappointed if you look only to secondary tribes for them. If you are looking to secondary tribes to tell you what to believe about yourself, you will be believing lies. Jesus never expected to find himself in his secondary tribes. He already knew who he was based on his primary tribes. Being in the Imago Dei and being imitators of Christ, we have the exact same primary tribes as Jesus. What are they?

The Trinity

Jesus existed in a mysterious three-person tribe from eternity past. The early church fathers used the Greek word *perichoresis* when talking about the relationship between the Father, Son, and Holy Spirit. The prefix *peri* means "around" (like perimeter), and the root *choresis* means "movement" (like choreography). The Trinity is like a holy, perfectly-choreographed dance where the dancers, without losing their individual identities, are in such harmony that "when one weeps, the others taste the salt."[2] Jesus could move on this earth as one who belonged while not belonging because he was grounded in this primary tribal identity. He gained ultimate identity from his union within the Trinity, so he was not drawn into an unhealthy attachment to his earthly tribes. He was not detached from the sting of betrayal or the sorrow of loss. He felt every human relational emotion. However, he often separated himself from

---

[2] Kruger C. Baxter, *The Great Dance: The Christian Vision Revisited* (Chicago: Perichoresis Press, 2000), Introduction, Kindle Edition.

the crowd to remind himself his true tribe was not of this earth.

How is the Trinity one of our primary tribes? Simply put, we are invited to join the dance. You may be thinking this sounds like heresy, but when you read the Bible through this lens, it will become abundantly clear that from Genesis to Revelation, God's whole point of creating and rescuing humans is to be close to us and to include us in his tribe! Read the excerpts from John 14 below and notice how many times Jesus used the phrase "in me" or "with me" to describe how he longs for a relationship with us. Also, note the *perichoresis* of the Father, Son, and Holy Spirit in this chapter. See Jesus's invitation to us to join the dance through faith in him.

> Do not let your hearts be troubled. You believe in God; believe also in me. My Father's house has many rooms; if that were not so, would I have told you that I am going there to prepare a place for you? And if I go and prepare a place for you, I will come back and take you *to be with me that you also may be where I am*. You know the way to the place where I am going.
>
> Thomas said to him, "Lord, we don't know where you are going, so how can we know the way?"
>
> Jesus answered, "I am the way and the truth and the life. No one comes to the Father except through me. *If you really know me, you will know my Father as well*. From now on, you do know him and have seen him."
>
> Philip said, "Lord, show us the Father and that will be enough for us."

Jesus answered: "Don't you know me, Philip, even after I have been among you such a long time? Anyone who has seen me has seen the Father. How can you say, 'Show us the Father'? Don't you believe that *I am in the Father, and that the Father is in me*? The words I say to you I do not speak on my own authority. Rather, it is the Father, *living in me*, who is doing his work. Believe me when I say that *I am in the Father and the Father is in me*; or at least believe on the evidence of the works themselves. Very truly I tell you, whoever believes in me will do the works I have been doing, and they will do even greater things than these, because I am going to the Father. And I will do whatever you ask in my name, so that the Father may be glorified in the Son. You may ask me for anything in my name, and I will do it.

If you love me, keep my commands. And I will ask the Father, and he will give you another advocate to help you and be with you forever—the Spirit of truth. The world cannot accept him, because it neither sees him nor knows him. *But you know him, for he lives with you and will be in you.* I will not leave you as orphans; *I will come to you.* Before long, the world will not see me anymore, but you will see me. *Because I live, you also will live.* On that day you will realize that *I am in my Father, and you are in me, and I am in you.* Whoever has my commands and keeps them is the one who loves me. *The one who loves me will be loved by my Father, and I too will love them and show myself to them. . .*

Anyone who loves me will obey my teaching. My Father will love them, and *we will come to them and make our home with them.* Anyone who does not love me will not obey my teaching. These words you hear are not my own; they belong to the Father who sent me.

All this I have spoken while still with you. But the Advocate, the Holy Spirit, whom the Father will send in my name, will teach you all things and will remind you of everything I have said to you. Peace I leave with you; my peace I give you. I do not give to you as the world gives. Do not let your hearts be troubled and do not be afraid."[3]

I love the part of this exchange where Philip says, "Lord, show us the Father, and that will be enough for us." I must admit I sometimes feel like Philip. The intimacy Jesus wants with us is almost uncomfortable. Knowing us, living with us, living in us, coming to us, loving us, making his home with us. It is almost too much to bear, yet this is the dance of intimacy he is inviting us to join. In this dance, we will be fully known, accepted, and loved. In this tribe, we will find purpose and belonging.

The Family of God

The Trinity was the primary tribe Jesus belonged to from eternity past. However, when he came to earth, he created another primary tribe, threw himself into it wholeheartedly, and then invited us to do the same. This tribe is, of course, the family of God that began

---

[3] John 14:1–21, 23–27 NIV, emphasis added

with the first twelve disciples (whom Jesus called brothers[4]), grew to include hundreds of followers,[5] and when Jesus returned to heaven, grew exponentially to become the worldwide Church. If you are a Jesus follower, you are a de facto member of this primary tribe. The New Testament uses the word "family" or "household" to describe the church more than any other metaphor.

> Respect everyone, and love your Christian brothers and sisters. (1 Peter 2:17a)

> Keep on loving one another as brothers and sisters. (Hebrews 13:1)

> Therefore, as we have opportunity, let us do good to all people, especially to those who belong to the family of believers. (Galatians 6:10)

> So now you Gentiles are no longer strangers and foreigners. You are citizens along with all of God's holy people. You are members of God's family. (Ephesians 2:19)

You are in the family-of-God tribe, whether you like it or not. You know people say when you get married that you are marrying "into the family"? In a sense, when you were adopted by God, you were adopted "into the family." You now have a bunch of diverse people you get to call brothers and sisters. When you identify as a Christ follower, you are now shoulder to shoulder with other Christ followers who worship and love God, love and care for each other,

---

[4] Matthew 12:48–50
[5] John 4:1

and have a common goal of reflecting his image to the world.

Big C, Little c

Just like every family can be described as both extended and immediate, the church can also be described broadly and narrowly. The broad description, which we will call the Big-C church, includes all Christians—past, present, and future. The narrow description is the local or little-c church. All Christians are part of the worldwide, Big-C church family. The Apostles' Creed calls it the "holy catholic church." We can think of this tribe as being like a wide river that has been flowing for generations. When you place your faith in Christ, you jump in and join the flow. When you participate in communion every week, like our church does, you are participating in a sacred ritual set in motion by Jesus himself and carried out by Christians all over the planet.

We can also think of the global Christian tribe as being like a giant, colorful patchwork quilt, where each piece beautifully portrays the image of Jesus. If you've ever traveled overseas, you know how amazing it is to hear hymns you know sung in another language and to see how different cultures worship the same God in their unique way. The unity we have in Christ breaks every cultural and social barrier. Heaven will be an enormous multicultural worship service where people from every tribe and nation will "confess that Jesus Christ is Lord, to the glory of God the Father."[6]

---

[6] Philippians 2:11

The next line of the Apostles' Creed states that we also believe in "the communion of saints." I get a warm fuzzy feeling thinking about the global unity we have in Christ in general terms, but that fuzzy feeling starts to fade when it comes down to the nitty gritty of developing true community with the Jesus followers who live near me. It's like one of the characters in *The Brothers Karamazov* said: "The more I love humanity in general, the less I love man in particular."[7]

Before he left this earth, Jesus set up the small-c, local church as his method for not only carrying out his mission of reconciliation to the world but also for the sanctification of its individual members. We cannot read the Epistles of the New Testament without coming to the conclusion that personal growth happens best within this family.

> From him the whole body, joined and held together by every supporting ligament, grows and builds itself up in love, as each part does its work. (Ephesians 4:16)

> Therefore, as God's chosen people, holy and dearly loved, clothe yourselves with compassion, kindness, humility, gentleness, and patience . . . . And over all these virtues put on love, which binds them all together in perfect unity. (Colossians 3:12, 14)

> Finally, all of you, live in harmony with one another; be sympathetic, love as brothers, be compassionate and humble. (1 Peter 3:8)

---

[7] Fyodor Dostoevsky, *The Brothers Karamazov* (New York: Barnes and Noble Classics, 2004), 61.

You can be a member of the family-of-God tribe but not enjoy the full benefits of membership. If you are not committed to a local church family, you are missing out on the opportunity to be challenged and changed by other Christians. You are also missing the opportunity to challenge and change your brothers and sisters.

I know it is messy. There are brothers and sisters who are hard to love. You will get hurt. You will be frustrated. You will want to walk away. However, if you do, you will not understand the blessings that come from laying yourself down for someone else, humbly loving someone who disagrees with you, walking through sin and reconciliation with a brother or sister, giving and receiving help in desperate times, and much more. If you do not have a local church family, go find one. Find one that believes the core tenets of the faith and aligns closest to your expression of faith, but don't be picky about music style, church décor, or programs you may not like. Don't bail on the church the first time you get your feelings hurt. Commit yourself to the family and participate in the little-c tribe.

To imitate Jesus, we must only look to our primary tribes to tell us what to believe about ourselves. When we place our faith in Jesus and become a "new creation,"[8] we join the everlasting *perichoresis* Trinity dance. Simultaneously, we are joined by millions of dancers—past, present, and future—who form our primary tribes: the family of God, both the Big C and the little c. All our other tribes—race, gender, socioeconomics, education, politics—are secondary tribes

---

[8] 2 Corinthians 5:17

that cannot give us a full understanding of who we are. We are children of God[9] first and foremost, and in union with our brothers and sisters as part of the family of God, the Church.

Don't Quit on Family!

You may be a bit skeptical of my assertion that the family of God is a primary tribe. This is probably because you've been hurt by the church. You jumped into a local small-c family, identified with them for a season of your life, and experienced the pain of being unseen, unheard, judged, or even ousted by this supposed family. Or maybe you're having a hard time seeing the church as a primary tribe because you've been disillusioned by it. You threw yourself into the mission and vision of a local church with gusto but, with time, you came to see the corruption in the leadership or in the mission itself and felt you had no choice but to walk out into a tribe-less wilderness.

These hurts are bound to happen in a fallen world, but too many people are giving up on participating with their fellow family members, and some are even shying away from identifying themselves as Christians because of the bad behavior of some who claim Christ. How can we avoid the temptation to abandon our tribe? There are three mentalities to avoid both individually and collectively if you want to enjoy long-term connection with the family of God on earth.

First, do not let anything other than Jesus be the unifying common ground for your community—not an affinity, a cause, a denomination, a set of values,

---

[9] John 1:12

or a status symbol. When we unify around Jesus-plus-anything-else, we run into the same issues of arrogance and exclusion that plague many of our secondary tribes. While you are committed to your small-c church family, you must never forget you are also part of the Large-C church, which includes millions of people who are very different from you. It grieves me to see churches from rival denominations bicker and compete with one another. We may not run the same plays, but we are on the same team. Or, to stick with the family metaphor, we may have more in common with our immediate family, but that doesn't mean we can look down our noses at those crazy second cousins.

Second, do not look to your Christian brothers and sisters to provide love only God can provide. It can be easy, especially if you come from a dysfunctional family, to forget the church is not God but simply fellow brothers and sisters under God the Father. Yes, the family takes care of each other, but if love and acceptance from other humans is the reason you joined your church tribe, you will forever be disappointed. Through the years, I have seen many people come to church with the expectation that all their relational needs will be met there. After a few years of trying to fill up their buckets with love from the leadership and others, they leave hurt and angry and then go from that church to another where they repeat the same pattern. Was there more the church could do to meet their needs? Probably. However, I can't help but wonder what the church would look like if everyone filled up with Christ's love before church on Sunday, then let that love spill onto everyone around them.

Third, do not let secondary tribal lines divide the family. The family-of-God tribe takes priority over all others. It is okay to be identified with a lot of different secondary tribes, but only one of those tribes should give you your actual identity. This should help clear up confusion in politics. You are an American (or another nationality), yes, but you are a Christian first. You are a Democrat/Republican/Libertarian, yes, but you are a Christian first. Don't shy away from discussing politics with your Christian brothers and sisters, but do so with the understanding that God is your Father as well as theirs, Jesus is your brother as well as theirs, and you share the same Holy Spirit who dwells in every believer.

New Glasses

When my husband was in seminary, one of his professors asserted that we all come to the Bible wearing glasses. We read it through a different lens depending on our preconceptions and interpretative framework. It is the same with your own story. When you take off the glasses of your secondary tribes and put on the glasses of your primary tribes, you begin to see your story in a whole new light. What will you see when you read your story through new glasses?

First, you will see a level playing field. Being part of the family of God is the great equalizer. Galatians 3:26–28 says, "You are all sons of God through faith in Christ Jesus, for all of you who were baptized into Christ have clothed yourselves with Christ. There is neither Jew nor Greek, slave nor free, male nor female, for you are all one in Christ Jesus." When you join God's family, he gives you a new set of clothes that overlays gender, class, nationality, occupation, and every other tribe that once defined you. You might have been marginalized and overlooked because of your earthly tribes, but not in your family-of-God tribe. You might have been honored and privileged simply because you were born into the right earthly tribe, but in God's family, everyone is just as honored and privileged as you. You are no better or worse than anyone else in the tribe. We have all been brought into the family through the unmerited mercy and grace of God our Father.

Second, through the lens of your primary tribes, you will see that you are—and have always been—fully accepted. Although you did nothing to deserve this acceptance (which should keep you humble), you are completely accepted. This should give you confidence. As we discussed in the previous chapter, much of the damage left by our original tribes had to do with a feeling of never fitting in or of not quite belonging. In God's tribe, there is no such thing as not belonging. As a member of God's family, you have special status. You have been given all the rights and inheritance a son or daughter deserves. This acceptance into the family should motivate you, in turn, to offer acceptance and love to every brother and sister in the family.

Finally, and above all, when we read our stories through the glasses of acceptance and belonging in God's family, we gain eternal perspective. Unlike all of your secondary tribes, your place in God's family is FOREVER. If your candidate did not win an election, if your state passed a law you don't like, if your Christian viewpoint is being mocked by the media, if your country is changing to become more secular and diverse, if your race or gender tribe is being discrimi-nated against, if you decide to change political parties or church affiliations or neighborhoods, your primary tribal identity remains firm. Nothing that happens to you on this earth can change the fact you are a son or daughter in the family of God. Do not wring your hands in fear of losing your tribal identity. You are a sojourner on this earth. Your permanent home is waiting for you when your feet leave this earth.

Reflection Questions

1. When we learn to give precedence to our primary tribes, we are able to see our secondary tribes for what they are—places to find belonging, affinity, and purpose, but *not* identity.

    Fill in the blanks: I believed I was _____ because of my earliest tribes, but now I know I am _____ because God has adopted me into his family.

2. Do you rely too heavily on your tribes for acceptance and affirmation? Are you at home wherever you find yourself? If you can't imagine who you would be without tribal identification, ask God to show you that you are already fully accepted and affirmed. Ask him to give you wisdom and courage to abandon any unhealthy tribal affiliations or the ability to engage tribes with the mindset of Jesus.

9

THE STORY OF THE VOICES
YOU LISTEN TO

A word is dead when it is said some say. I say it
just begins to live that day.
– Emily Dickinson[1]

A life that is burdened with expectations is a heavy
life. Its fruit is sorrow and disappointment.
– Douglas Adams[2]

L et's recap a bit before we dive into this chapter. Our identity is what we believe to be true
about ourselves. It informs our emotions and
motivates our actions. These beliefs are often rooted
in our early experiences and are difficult—but not impossible—to change. The three things that contribute
most to our identity formation are the love we respond
to, the tribes we belong to, and the voices we listen to.
We've tackled the first two contributing factors in the
previous chapters, and we've discussed how God can
change our false identity beliefs through his love and
his tribes. In this chapter, we will discuss the final
thread to our identity story: the voices we listen to.

---

[1] Emily Dickinson, *The Complete Poems of Emily Dickinson*
(n.p.: Wilder Publications, Inc., 2014), Chapter 3, Kindle Edition.
[2] Douglas Adams, *Long Dark Tea-Time of the Soul* (New York:
Pocket Books, 2014), Chapter 4, Kindle Edition.

We live in a noisy age. Everywhere we turn, someone is trying to get our attention, to convince us we need what they're selling, to get us to care about their cause, to educate us about our health or parenting. There is no shortage of voices shouting at us every day, but what are they saying about identity?

You've been taking in identity information your whole life whether you realize it or not. Here's how it works. Someone says something about who you are or who you should be. You subconsciously look for second opinions on that information. When you've heard that same message from multiple sources—or even from the same source multiple times—you begin internalizing that message and it slowly becomes part of your identity. In time you believe those things are true. Those beliefs inform your emotions and become the motivation of your thoughts and actions.

Let's follow that trail with a tangible example. A young boy is called a wimp by his coach when he lets pain from an injury keep him from playing. He subconsciously thinks, "I don't want to be a wimp. I will do my best to hide pain." As he grows, he hears other people say the same thing. His relatives, teachers, and peers all mention in one way or another that real men don't show pain, whether physical or emotional. Everyone compliments him on his toughness. He begins to believe it and it becomes part of his identity. Armed with the belief that he is impervious to the weakness of emotion, he has confidence in social settings. He chooses to associate with other tough guys who use derisive terms for boys who show emotion. There is a nagging feeling in his soul that he must maintain his toughness in order to be accepted and valued. He begins to obsess about building up his physical strength to prove to himself and to the world he is not a sissy. At some point, though, he realizes he cannot live up to these expectations. Rather than blame these excessive expectations, he blames himself. He is ashamed when his mom gets cancer and he breaks down publicly. He can't admit he is not holding it together when job stress threatens to overwhelm him. He hides behind bravado but inside feels like a failure. Depression leads to drinking, which leads to more depression, and down the spiral he tumbles.

There is a way to fix the problem of bad messaging, and that is to replace it by working in reverse. Start with the action (in this case, drinking), dig down to the emotion (depression), discover the motive (feelings of failure), and find out what belief is driving that motive (unmet expectation). If that belief came from the repeated messages he received throughout his life, he needs to replace those messages with different ones.

There are two basic categories of identity messaging we absorb throughout our lives. One is the "you are" (or "you are not") statements. The other is the "you should" (or "you should not") statements.

Negative "You Are's"

"Sticks and stones may break my bones but words will never hurt me." Have you ever heard a more nonsensical statement? Bones heal much more quickly than brains and hearts. Some of us never recover from the word-wounds we have received. I asked my Facebook friends to share with me one phrase they heard from an early age that stuck with them throughout their lives. Here's a sampling of the "You are" statements:

- "Remember, you are not white. Don't try to fit in with white people."
- "You have a real mean streak."
- "I don't compliment you because I don't want you to get a big head."
- "You don't have much to say. You'll make a man very happy one day."
- "You will never be anything."
- "You'll never make it in college."
- "You are not welcome here."
- "Why are you being such a snob?"
- "You will never be good at math."
- "Why are you so quiet?"
- "You dance like a bull in a china shop."
- "What is wrong with you?"
- "You always look mad."
- "You can't do _____. You're a girl."
- "No man is ever going to want you."
- "You are nothing without your parents' blessing. God will only bless you if we do."
- "You're smart, but you have no common sense."
- "Your daughter is a stupid little girl."
- "I don't know what he sees in you."
- "Your son is a hopeless case."
- "You are a larger-framed woman."
- "You are skin and bones."
- "Your legs are too long."
- "You are way too sensitive."
- "You are bossy."

What phrase would you add to the list? I have a friend whose father used to repeat the phrases "How could you be so foolish?" or "How could you be so stupid?" every time he messed up. He admits he has spent his entire life trying to prove to himself and the world how "not-foolish" he is. Another friend had a mom who would tell her, "You're not a natural beauty. You should never leave the house without makeup." This little phrase has caused her to believe she was never good enough unless she altered who she was in some way. Research shows that children who ingest repeated negative verbal communication grow up to be adults who have limited emotional intelligence, rejection sensitivity, and a crippling self-critique that assumes every bad thing they experience is due to a character flaw.[3] Negative "You are's" can be like wet cement, freezing us into a permanent negative opinion of ourselves.

Positive "You Are's"

What about positive "You are's?" Can those sometimes have negative effects on identity? One of my friends said that being repeatedly told "You are so beautiful" caused her to attach her value to her looks. The phrase "You can be anything you want to be" made another friend feel like anything less than extraordinary was not good enough. In my life, being told I was talented and destined for great things had the same effect on me. What adults meant as positive

---

[3] Peg Streep, "The Enduring Pain of Childhood Verbal Abuse," *Psychology Today*, November 14, 2016, https://www.psychology today.com/blog/tech-support/201611/the-enduring-pain-childhood-verbal-abuse.

reinforcement was heard through children's ears as pressure and expectation.

At this point, you may be wondering if there is anything you *can* say to a child or friend that would not be harmful. There is! The right type of praise goes a long way to boost confidence and security. Carol Dweck's book *Mindset* asserts there are two basic mindsets that determine whether or not you will thrive. The fixed mindset is when you believe your qualities and successes are predetermined based on genetics. The growth mindset is when you believe success is directly linked to effort. People with a fixed mindset must prove themselves, hide deficiencies, seek out people who will affirm and not challenge them, and avoid experiences that will stretch them. People with a growth mindset seek ways to improve themselves, fix deficiencies, welcome negative feedback as learning opportunities, and relish new experiences even if they will be challenging. Raising four children, I have to admit that mindset is somewhat innate. Some of my children are more naturally inclined from birth to one mindset or another. However, as Dweck points out, I can reinforce mindset by the quality of my praise.

> Listen for the messages in the following examples:
>
> > "You learned that so quickly! You're so smart!"
> >
> > "Look at that drawing. Martha, is he the next Picasso or what?"
> >
> > "You're so brilliant, you got an A without even studying."

If you're like most parents, you hear these as supportive, esteem-boosting messages. But listen more closely. See if you can hear another message. It's the one that children hear:

> "If I don't learn something quickly, I'm not smart."

> "I shouldn't try drawing anything hard or they'll see I'm no Picasso."

> "I'd better quit studying or they won't think I'm brilliant."[4]

In study after study, kids who were praised for their natural ability performed lower than kids who were praised for their effort. Not only did they perform lower, they felt worse when they failed, and they made excuses or tried to hide their failure. When praised for effort, however, children were not only more apt to try harder the next time, they actually outperformed those praised for ability. Adults do not realize how deeply imbedded the wrong type of praise sinks into a child's psyche. What happens when the boy who is praised for his athletic ability gets cut from a team? Or when the girl praised for her leadership ability gets thrown into a leadership role that overwhelms her? Or when the kind girl realizes she has a selfish vein when she steals her best friend's boyfriend? Identity crises ensue and confidence plummets. Parents and teachers assume the only way to get a kid back to their confident self is to compliment them some more, and now we have a generation of praise-addicted (and ironically less confident) young adults.

---

[4] Carol Dweck, *Mindset: The New Psychology of Success* (New York: Ballantine Books, 2008), 174–175.

Adults are not the only ones responsible for our insatiable appetite for affirmation. Social media has fueled the praise addiction by creating platforms for us to create exaggerated versions of ourselves. We post filtered pictures and then wait for the positive feedback to pour in as a determinant of our self-worth. In an excellent article on the impact of social media on identity, psychologist Jim Taylor asserts our culture is in the midst of a seismic shift from internal to external drivers. External contributors have always played a role in the development of our self-identity, he says, "but they had been, up until recently, partners of sorts with our own internal contributors to self-identity. But now the sheer ubiquity and force of the latest technological advances has taken that influence and turned its volume up to a deafening roar . . . The goal for many now in their use of social media becomes how they can curry acceptance, popularity, status, and, by extension, self-esteem through their profiles and postings. Self-awareness and self-expression give way to impression management and self-promotion."[5]

The "You are's" you have heard, both positive and negative, from adults, peers, and social media have probably contributed more than you realize to your beliefs about yourself.

---

[5] Jim Taylor, "Technology: Is Technology Stealing our (Self) Identities?" *Psychology Today*, July 27, 2011, https://www.psychologytoday.com/blog/the-power-prime/201107/technology-is-technology-stealing-our-self-identities.

"You Should's"

Another equally damaging category of identity-form-ing messages we receive are the "You should's." Whereas the "You are" labels leave you stuck in a pre-determined identity, the "You should" statements do allow for change, but often the change is based on becoming who someone else wants you to be, not nec-essarily who God wants you to be. Here are real examples from friends of mine.

- "You can do better."
- "You talk too much."
- "You must have done something to de-serve getting slapped."
- "You shouldn't eat that or you will be fat like me."
- "Children are to be seen and not heard."
- "Stop acting like a sissy and face your problems like a man."
- "Don't talk. Nobody cares what you have to say."
- "Smart girls don't get the boys."
- "You'll never be a good employee. You move too slow."
- "Your house is messy. I feel bad for your husband."
- "No one wants to hear about that subject. It's boring."
- "I'd sooner have God take my children to heaven than have them turn their backs on him."

Do you hear the "You should's" in each of these statements? My mom grew up in a German household where cleanliness was next to godliness and laziness next to the pits of hell. She instilled those values into us by yanking the sheets off our sleepy, warm bodies at 7:00 a.m. every Saturday to wash them, often whilst singing a cheery "Good Morning" tune. If she ever caught us sitting around, she'd give us a job to do, so we became skilled at acting busy whenever we heard her approaching. She loved those verses in Proverbs about behaving like the industrious ant and not the sloth. When we finally got a TV, she bemoaned the hours wasted in front of the screen when we could have been productive. This may seem like a silly example, but those messages caused me to set the bar of activity for myself at an almost unattainable level. I felt that if I didn't stay busy, I would be the very thing my mom most despised. For many years of my life, I found my value in the fullness of my calendar and the items checked off my to-do list.

My husband's dad used to tell his children they were put on this earth to "do great things for God." This mantra has been a motivator at times in his life, but mostly it made him feel like he was failing. Swiss psychologist Alice Miller says this about the enduring effects of parental "You should's."

> Many people suffer all their lives from this oppressive feeling of guilt, the sense of not having lived up to their parents' expectations. This feeling is stronger than any intellectual insight they might have, that it is not a child's task or duty to satisfy his parents' needs. No argument can overcome these guilt feelings, for they have their

beginnings in life's earliest periods, and from that they derive their intensity and obduracy.[6]

Think about all the "You should" or "You shouldn't" messages you've heard from teachers, parents, coaches, and friends. How have you adjusted your words, thoughts, or actions to fit the molds created for you? What do you feel the worst guilt about? Do you feel that guilt because you aren't living up to someone else's expectations of you?

Of course, unless you've been living in a cave or a commune, you have also been massively affected by media "You should" messages your entire life.

> Popular culture manufactures "portraits" of who it wants us to be. Tapping into our most basic needs to feel good about ourselves, accepted, and attractive, popular culture tells us what we should believe about ourselves. The problem is that the self-identity that is shaped by popular culture serves its own best interests rather than what is best for us. Additionally, self-identity is no longer self-identity, meaning derived from the self, but rather is an identity projected onto us by popular culture and in no way an accurate reflection of who we really are.[7]

Almost all the television, movie, magazine, and advertising identity messaging we ingest can be boiled down to these two words: *not enough*. You are not rich

---

[6] Alice Miller, *The Drama of the Gifted Child* (New York: Basid Books, 2007), Chapter 3, Kindle Edition.

[7] Jim Taylor, "Is Technology Stealing our (Self) Identities?" *Psychology Today*, July 27, 2011, https://www.psychology today.com/blog/the-power-prime/201107/technology-is-technology-stealing-our-self-identities.

enough, smart enough, beautiful enough, cultured enough, traveled enough, popular enough, fit enough, working hard enough. You are not a good enough wife, husband, parent, teacher, friend, employee, Christian, student, child. You do not have enough. You do not do enough. *You* are not enough.

Brené Brown, in her book *Daring Greatly*, calls this the problem of scarcity.

> Scarcity thrives in a culture where everyone is hyper-aware of lack. Everything from safety and love to money and resources feels restricted and lacking. We spend inordinate amounts of time calculating how much we have, want, and don't have, and how much everyone else has, needs, and wants. What makes the constant assessing and comparing so self-defeating is that we are often comparing our lives, our marriages, our families, and our communities to unattainable, media-driven visions of perfection, or we're holding up our reality against our own fictional account of how great someone else has it.[8]

When you are convinced you are not enough, you fill in the gaps with implicit "You should's" in order to achieve "enough." Pile up enough of these "You should's" and pretty soon you are just a walking mass of underachieving guilt, anxiety, depression, or addiction.

Really, this not-enough message is not new. It was the lie told to Eve when Satan introduced the

---

[8] Brené Brown, *Daring Greatly: How the Courage to Be Vulnerable Transforms the Way We Live, Love, Parent, and Lead* (New York: Penguin Random House, 2012), Chapter 1, Kindle Edition.

tantalizing possibility that there might be a greener pasture on the other side of that forbidden fruit. The human race is universally susceptible to these seeds of discontentment, sown every day and in every way by the media. The truth is, the not-enough lie is already present in every human heart. All the advertisers and movie makers have to do is exploit it for their own gain. We are ripe for the picking.

Don't Kill the Messenger

In the next chapter, we will get into more detail on how to hear these "You are" and "You should" messages through the filter of God's voice, but I want to first acknowledge that the problem is not entirely the messages or the message-bearers. Remember all the way back to chapter four when we talked about the three enemies we all encounter as we try to live out the Imago Dei?

First, we are dealing with our *sin nature*, which causes us to twist and warp the words we hear into long-lasting identity statements. Second, we are fighting our very real spiritual enemy, *Satan*, whose job is to deceive us by twisting words said to and about us into identity lies. Third, we are contending with our *story*, which is what this book is primarily focused on. Sometimes the messages we heard were intended to bruise and break us and fill us with self-doubt. For the most part, however, our parents, teachers, and friends did not intend any harm when they spoke those words to us. When you add the other two enemies—sin and Satan—into the mix, those comments, compliments, and corrections can twist into lies we tell ourselves for years, lies that hold us back from becoming all God created us to be.

I want to also recognize the important, positive role of all the messengers in our lives. I am forever grateful to my parents, teachers, mentors, and friends for all the empowering, corrective, loving, affirming, and instructive identity-forming messages spoken to me through the years. If it weren't for them, I might not have had the courage to write this book. Please don't let the damaging impact of the "You are" and "You should" statements make you shy away from speaking words of life to your children, students, and peers. Proverbs says, "faithful are the wounds of a friend"[9] and compares a word "fitly spoken" to "apples of gold in pictures of silver."[10] As long as they are in line with God's truth and said in love, "You are's" and "You should's" can be incredibly powerful.

---

[9] Proverbs 27:6
[10] Proverbs 25:11

Reflection Questions

1. Take a minute to think about the messages you've received from authority figures, peers, and media. You cannot help but be influenced by the millions of voices you hear throughout your lifetime. See if you can identify some key core beliefs about yourself that have come from these messages. Fill in the blanks:

   I was told I was _____, and I believed it.

   I was told I should _____, and I am still trying to be/do that, even though I know those are not God's expectations.

2. Now, take it one step further and ask yourself if these identity statements are holding you back from being who God created you to be.

   In the next chapter, we will discuss how to drown out those negative identity voices with the voice of the One who knows and loves us best.

10

THE STORY OF GOD'S VOICE

It is written: "Man shall not live on bread alone, but on every word that comes from the mouth of God."
— Matthew 4:4

Many voices ask for our attention. There is a voice that says, "Prove that you are a good person." Another voice says, "You'd better be ashamed of yourself." There also is a voice that says, "Nobody really cares about you," and one that says, "Be sure to become successful, popular, and powerful." But underneath all these often very noisy voices is a still, small voice that says, "You are my Beloved, my favor rests on you." That's the voice we need most of all to hear. To hear that voice, however, requires special effort; it requires solitude, silence, and a strong determination to listen.
— Henri Nouwen[1]

D o you remember the old car radio dials? For those who are too young to remember, I'll do my best to describe this prehistoric technology. Once upon a time, people did not listen to their iPhones in the car. They listened to something called a car radio. In these old cars, radios didn't have

---

[1] Henri J.M. Nouwen, *Bread for the Journey: A Daybook of Wisdom and Faith* (San Francisco: HarperCollins, 2007), January 13, Kindle Edition.

fancy buttons you could push to search for a station. No, you had to turn a knob to find your favorite station. Unlike the old TV dials that clicked when you turned them, however, you had to slowly turn the radio tuner until you found just the right frequency in order to clear the static.

Now, just imagine there is a car radio that could play every single station on the planet, but there is only one station you want to listen to. You painstakingly ease the dial clockwise, trying to find the one station out of millions that is broadcasting the music you want to hear. For a split second, you somehow manage to find the station, but you overturn the dial by a hair and it is lost again in the static. That is how it feels sometimes to try to listen to God's voice amidst the cacophony of voices around you. Yet, in order to replace the bad messages that have become cemented into your identity, you have to hear what your Creator God has to say to you. You must learn to tune into *his* voice, believe what *he* says is true, and then turn down the rest of the noise.

Jesus was always telling people to turn down the "You are" and "You should" labels of the world and tune in to him. In the story of the Samaritan woman in John 4, he looks past three of these labels in order to just converse with her. One, she was a Samaritan. Jews and Samaritans hated each other. Two, she was a woman. Men in those days did not talk to women publicly unless they were a family member or close friend. Three, she was a social outcast. She was at the well at noon, alone, when all the other women of the town had already come and gone.

Jesus smashes through all of these barriers when he *speaks* to her. I imagine her looking over her shoulder when he says, "Will you give me a drink?" and wondering who he is talking to. When she realizes he is talking to her, she doesn't hop to it and get him a drink right away. She is incredulous.

"Why are you talking to me?" she asks. "You know you're not supposed to."

He responds by essentially saying, "Tune out the voices telling you you're not worth my attention. Tune in to *my* voice." Not only does he speak to her, he offers her living water that will quench her thirst for love and affirmation that five husbands have failed to fulfill. "You've been drinking out of the wrong well all these years. Drink my water, and you will not be thirsty for the cheap substitutes that will never satisfy."

What is this living water Jesus offered her and still offers us today? It is an identity grounded in the belief that we are not defined by any voice but his. We are who *he* says we are.

Who does God Say You Are?

God has a lot to say about you. You just have to tune in and listen. Read this list out loud. If you find any of these statements difficult to believe, look them up.

> I am a son or daughter of God (John 1:12)
> I am pure and holy (1 Corinthians 1:30)
> I am a new creation (2 Corinthians 5:17)
> I am blameless (Ephesians 1:4)
> I am God's masterpiece (Ephesians 2:10)
> I am loved and chosen (1 Thessalonians 1:4)
> I am fully known (Psalm 139:1–6)
> I am never alone (Psalm 139:7–12)

I am intimately woven together by my Creator
(Psalm 139:13–16)

I am uniquely gifted by God to glorify him (Romans 12:6)

I am an essential part in the body of Christ
(1 Corinthians 12:27)

I am forgiven (Psalm 103:3)

I am God's treasured possession (Deuteronomy
26:18, 1 Peter 2:9)

I am predestined, called, justified, and glorified
by God (Romans 8:30)

I am accepted (Romans 15:7)

I am part of a royal priesthood (I have direct
access to God through Christ) (1 Peter 2:9)

I am clothed in Christ's righteousness (Galatians 3:27)

I am of equal value to every other Christian
(Galatians 3:28)

I am not my own, but have been bought by
Christ (2 Corinthians 6:19–20)

I am dead to my sin (Romans 6:11)

I am alive in Christ (Galatians 2:20)

I am a friend of God (John 15:15)

I am highly valued by God (Matthew 6:26)

I am crowned with glory and honor (Psalm 8:5)

I am free from condemnation (Romans 8:1)

I am an heir of eternal life (Romans 8:17)

I am the light of the world and the salt of the
earth (Matthew 5:13–14)

I am a winner (Romans 8:37)

I am designed for good works (Ephesians 2:10)

I am dependent on God for everything (Acts
17:28, Romans 11:36)

I am given everything I need to live a godly life
(2 Peter 1:3)

Guess what? This list is not exhaustive. God has many more things to say to you. You will find them on the pages of his Word, but you must first turn down the voices of the world around you. He will not shout above the noise. It takes time spent in quiet to be able to hear what he wants to tell you.

When my second son was born, his pediatrician thought she heard a murmur through her stethoscope at a routine checkup. She suggested we get an echocardiogram to verify, but it turned out to be nothing serious. Over the years, the simple rudimentary stethoscope, developed two hundred years ago, has saved thousands of lives, but only when it is used by trained ears. To the untrained ear, patient heartbeats heard through the stethoscope sound indistinguishable from each other. But to the doctor who is trained to hear the harmonics, overtones, and rhythmic irregularities, it is common to hear arrhythmia, murmurs, signs of congestive heart failure, and valve blockages.

In order to hear God's identity messages and apply them to our hearts, we must train our ears to distinguish his voice. As Henri Nouwen describes in *The Return of the Prodigal Son*, "I have to kneel before the Father, put my ear against his chest and listen, without interruption, to the heartbeat of God."[2] It will sometimes take years of tuning in to his voice and turning down the noisy world to believe his truth more than every other message.

---

[2] Henri J. M. Nouwen, *The Return of the Prodigal Son: A Story of Homecoming* (New York: Doubleday, 1994), 17.

Change Your Hearing

You might be wondering how simply reading and internalizing the "I am" statements God makes about you will help you tune out the messages you are being bombarded with in your everyday life. Tuning those voices out completely is impossible, but what if you could hear them differently? I have a musically gifted friend who hears color. When a certain note or chord is played, he envisions purple, green, orange, or blue. Scientists call this brain phenomenon "synesthesia" where the senses cross over and get mixed up with each other. Until recent years, it was thought synesthesia was the product of an overactive imagination. However, modern brain research has proven this mixing of the senses genuinely exists. While I cannot hear color (I wish I could!), I can train my heart and mind to hear differently.

When I am presented with information about myself, I can hear it in two ways. If my identity is wrapped up in what people think about me, I will hear criticism as a blow to my core and will be crushed or incensed by it. I will hear praise as affirmation of my identity and will be elated or inflated by it. The reason I respond this way is because I have given too much weight to those opinions. I have given them the power to shape my beliefs about myself. As we have learned from the previous chapters, this power to shape identity belongs not to them or even to me but only to God.

The better way to hear identity information is through the filter of God's opinion of me. If my identity is firmly grounded in the truth of God's unconditional love, I have two options when responding to outside voices. First, after I have determined they contradict

God's voice, I can ignore those voices. This is not an easy thing to do, especially when you love and respect the person who is giving you the message!

My friend, whose dad used to tell people he'd rather have his children in heaven than turn their backs on God, told me she spent years of her life afraid God would strike her dead if she disobeyed him in the least. It took a very long time for her to be able to ignore her father's voice, but she was finally able to do it by replacing it with God's.

Second, it is not only the negative messages we sometimes need to ignore. Praise can be just as important to block out. I'm not talking about having false humility and shunning compliments. I teach my children to accept a compliment with gratitude and grace. However, we need to be careful not to give too much power to human praise.

When we first started our church, several people told my husband, "You are such a great preacher. I wouldn't be surprised if your church explodes from 25 people to 1,000 in the first five years." Those people were trying to be encouraging, but those words were not helpful. If my husband's identity was firmly grounded in his acceptance by Christ, he could have ignored their words and continued on faithfully serving God without any thought to earthly success. However, since his identity was tied in large part to his performance, he took their praise and turned it into pressure. When our church didn't explode, he felt like a failure. It took several years for him to learn that God's standard of success was not the same as the world's, and that he was successful in God's eyes whether he had 25 or 2,500 in his congregation. After learning that important identity lesson, when people complimented his speaking or told him he would be a "big success," he could smile and say "thank you," then mentally ignore the compliment, knowing it had no bearing on his identity.

When we are hearing identity information correctly, the first appropriate response to those voices is to ignore them when they contradict God's voice. However, what if God wants to use the voices of the people in your life to change you for the better? When someone says something negative to or about you, the second appropriate response is to determine if it is true, even if only partially. If so, rather than being crushed or incensed, thank them for their input, walk away, and pray about their critique. While you pray, remind yourself your identity doesn't hinge on their opinion of you, but on God's. Seek to hear God's voice by reading his word and if you determine this is an area of your life that needs changing, humbly and in God's strength do the work to change. How refreshing would it be if we could all turn our critics into coaches? We could then thank God for using people to point out our flaws but still move through life in complete confidence that our core identity is unfazed by human critique.

There is perhaps no relationship where my identity has been challenged more than in my marriage. Coming into marriage, I thought of myself as a good person: responsible, loyal, patient, loving, kind (insert ironic laugh here). It only took about three days of marriage for that identity to be challenged. The first time my husband said something like, "You're really judgmental" or "You have anger issues," my response was not to thank him for his input. Instead, I swung back. Hard. "Oh yeah, well I wouldn't be angry if you didn't push my buttons!"

Thinking back now, I realize that in calling out my less-than-perfect behavior, he was challenging my belief about myself as a good person. It wasn't just my ego but my identity that was threatened. And it needed to be threatened! My belief about myself was false. God's truth about me (and everyone else) is that I am not a good person. I am a sinner. Fully loved and accepted, yes, but on Christ's merit, not my own. Understanding myself to be more of a sinner than I thought was not enjoyable, but it was necessary in order for me to learn to respond with humility to criticism. Now, with my identity rooted in the truth of the gospel (I am a sinner, a work in progress, but fully loved and accepted), I am not threatened by my husband's critique. I may not always agree with it, but I am able to see it as helpful, not harmful.

You might be the exact opposite of me, responding to critique with shame and self-loathing instead of pride and defensiveness. Your identity might not be "I am a good person," but "I am a bad person," and people's negative opinions of you only serve to reinforce that belief. You might stay in self-loathing and never change, or you might change like a chameleon to try to please everyone. Either way, in order to change your behavior, you have to change your belief. You must tune into what God says is true about you—you are fully loved, accepted, forgiven, and holy—in order to drown out the voices that are crippling you with shame. When you are faced with a negative opinion of yourself, rather than beating yourself up or quickly changing your behavior to please that person, take a step back. Ask God if it is true. Ask God to reveal if it is something he wants you to change. If so, begin the process of changing, but reject the notion that your identity has anything to do with your performance or with any person's opinion of you.

It is not possible—nor is it always beneficial—to fully tune out the "You are" and "You should" messages we receive. We can hear them differently, however. Henri Nouwen says, "As long as I remain in touch with the voice that calls me the Beloved, these questions and counsels are quite harmless. Parents, friends, and teachers, even those who speak to me through the media, are mostly very sincere in their concerns . . . But when I forget the voice of the first unconditional love, then these innocent suggestions can easily start dominating my life and pull me into the 'distant country.'"[3] When we are confident that God's opinion of us is the only true opinion, we can identify and ignore the untruths and welcome critique as an opportunity to grow more fully into the Imago Dei.

Two Portraits

Nervous Nicky

Nicky was a middle child of three.[4] Her older brother was a whiz kid who never had to study and graduated early from high school and college. Her younger sister was a born performer who could outshine Beyoncé, and she sang and danced her way to a fancy performing arts school. Nicky was shy, an

---

[3] Nouwen, *The Return*, 41.
[4] These are completely fictional characters, but I felt the need to put flesh and blood into these identity ideas so we could see ourselves in these people and our stories in theirs.

average student, not particularly talented or beautiful and, according to her best friend in fourth grade, "not very interesting." Her sixth-grade teacher called her a mouse when she spoke too softly during an oral report, and her soccer coach said she was slow after her opponent dribbled past her and scored. Her parents didn't say anything negative to Nicky growing up, but they definitely didn't pay as much attention to her as they did to her superstar siblings. Nicky graduated high school but didn't think she would do well in college, so she opted for a nursing assistant program at the community college. She had a group of friends to go to parties and concerts with, but one by one they moved away for college and eventually started getting married. She considered herself too shy and uninteresting to make new friends, so at thirty, she found herself living in an apartment, working a boring job, with her dogs as her only companions.

She desperately wanted her life to change, but because she had those beliefs about herself cemented in her brain, she felt stuck and powerless. Her only hope was for someone to come along and rescue her, so it is no surprise she fell for the first man who showed interest in her. He did not always treat her very well, but she was so overjoyed at not being alone that she overlooked his flaws and busied herself taking care of him. They got married and she threw herself headlong into being a good wife and homemaker. Nothing was ever good enough for her husband, but rather than blame him, she blamed herself. When he complained about a meal, to her ears, it was confirmation of the identity beliefs she already held about herself: "I am uninteresting." "I am not talented." Her efforts to please him spiraled into anxiety and panic attacks. At forty, she was alone again—divorced and medicated.

Confident Candace

Candace's family moved twelve times before she turned sixteen. Her dad was an abusive alcoholic and was out of the picture by the time she was ten. Before the divorce, though, Candace and her sister bore the brunt of their father's alcohol-fueled rage on several occasions. He told Candace she looked like a whore when she played dress up and wore her mother's lipstick. On more than one occasion, he told his daughters he wished they were sons because boys were "a little less useless." When Candace brought home a good report card in third grade he said, "It's a good thing you've got a good brain because you sure don't have much else." That good brain led Candace to graduate with honors and pursue a career in bioengineering. At twenty-four, she had a master's degree and was pursuing her doctorate, but her father's voice still rang in her ears: "A good brain is all you've got." She worked herself to the bone, never taking breaks, never having fun. A negative critique from a professor would land her in bed for a day, then she would throw herself even harder into her studies. It was vital she succeed at her career because she believed she was nothing without it. Then she met Garrett.

She had had a few boyfriends before Garrett, but she pushed them all away before it could get too serious. None of them were willing to pursue her like he was, to get past all the pushing, to uncover the deep insecurities carved into her identity by the voice of her father. Garrett introduced Candace to her heavenly

Father and helped her to tune into his voice. Slowly, she began the process of replacing her earthly father's critical voice with the adoring voice of God. Slowly, she started to believe she was much more than a brain. Slowly, she lost the need to prove her intelligence. Slowly, she began hearing critique from professors and work colleagues not as assaults on her identity, but as opportunities to grow. She never married Garrett, but is forever grateful to him for the gift of a life-changing relationship with God. She finally did get married at thirty, just like Nicky, but because she had been tuning into God's identity messages for five years, she was comfortable in her own skin. She chose a man who loved and respected her. By forty, she had two children, worked part time, and enjoyed the confidence that came from listening to the voice of her heavenly Father.

Do you see yourself, even a little bit, in either of these fictional characters? My hope for you after reading these stories is that you will no longer be the victim of your negative identity messages but will seek out the messages readily available to you in God's Word.

Cut and Paste

The only way to repair the damage done to your identity beliefs is to return to those old false messages and replace them with God's voice. Go back to the end of chapter ten where you wrote out the messages that had the biggest impact on your identity. First, determine whether that statement is true or false. If it is false, find a verse and write it out beside the statement. If possible, change the wording of the verse to the first person. Replace "You are worthless" with "I am God's treasured possession" (1 Peter 2:9). Replace "You have nothing to offer" with "I am uniquely gifted by God to glorify him" (Romans 12:6). Replace "You are a sinner" with "I have been forgiven" (Psalm 103:3). Replace "You are destined for great things" with "I am already a success in God's eyes" (Romans 8:37). Replace "You are not enough" with "I have everything I need" (2 Peter 1:3).

Now, when a destructive behavior or thought pops up, trace it all the way back to see if it has its roots in false identity messaging. If so, cut it out and paste in God's messaging. If you discipline yourself to hear God's voice above the noise and if you repeatedly replace those false messages, in time, you will see that destructive thought or behavior start to fade away.

Reflection Questions

1. How do you receive critique? If you become defensive, self-loathing, or avoidant when you are criticized, why do you think that is? How can you respond with humility and grace?

2. How do you receive praise? If you are generally low in confidence unless you are being praised, or if you turn praise into pressure, why do you think that is? How can you put praise in its proper place— nice but not necessary?

11

WHO ARE YOU?

"Wasn't I real before?" asked the little Rabbit.
"You were Real to the Boy," the Fairy said, "because
he loved you. Now you shall be Real to every one."
– Margery Williams[1]

This means that anyone who belongs to Christ has
become a new person. The old life is gone; a new
life has begun!
– 2 Corinthians 5:17 (NLT)

I love the Olympic Games. I'll never forget the awe
and pride I had watching Mary Lou Retton vault
and flip her way to an Olympic gold when I was
a girl. I love the pageantry of the opening and closing
ceremonies, the podiums bearing tearful medal-earn-
ers, and the unity and camaraderie of rooting for
Team USA. I love the biographical videos of individual
athletes, especially the ones who overcame tremendous odds just to be at the games. The bigger their
obstacles, the sweeter the victory.

I was thrilled to see a US diving duo win silver in
synchronized diving at the 2016 Rio summer games,
but I was even more thrilled to hear their final interview. When asked about the pressure he felt before

---

[1] Margery Williams, *The Velveteen Rabbit* (New York: Avon
Books, 1975), 38–39.

the dive, David Boudia answered, "When my mind is on this [the diving] and thinking I'm defined by this, my mind goes crazy. But we both know our identity is in Christ." Steele Johnson had a similar response. "I was going into this event knowing that my identity was rooted in Christ and not what the result of this competition is. That gave me peace and gave me ease, and let me enjoy the contest. If something went great, I was happy. If something didn't go great, I could still find joy."

I'm used to hearing athletes give props to God after a victory, but I had never heard anything like this. These guys were basically saying, "We refuse to believe that success in this competition is essential to our self-worth. God doesn't care whether we win or lose a medal. We are already winners in his eyes." I had to find out more about them. I came to find out this was David's third Olympics. After finishing in tenth place in Beijing in 2008, he became depressed, began drinking heavily, and contemplated suicide. In his despair, he reached out to a coach, who introduced him to Jesus. His life dramatically changed. For a while, he quit diving because it seemed insignificant compared to his newfound identity in Christ. He eventually returned to his sport a transformed person and went on to win gold in London in 2012. His diving partner, Steele Johnson, almost died when his head struck a platform at age twelve. That near-death experience put his diving dreams in eternal perspective. When he returned to diving, it was for love of the sport more than for the fame of success.

Knowing they were fully loved and accepted by God gave David and Steele the freedom to enjoy their sport and the motivation to succeed, not for the praise of the world but for the glory of God. Whereas once they had defined themselves by their victories and defeats, they now determined "Olympic Diver" would never be a good enough answer to the question "Who are you?"

Who are You?

"Who are you?" is one of the most important questions you will ever be asked. How you answer will determine the framework through which you see the world, interact with people, and make decisions. Author and theologian Henri Nouwen says there are three common "wrong answers" to this question that lead to anxiety, frustration, pride, and discontentment. They are "I am what I do," "I am what I have," and "I am what people think of me."[2]

"I am What I Do"

If you asked David Boudia or Steele Johnson, "Who are you?" you would not hear "I am an Olympic diver," but rather "I am a beloved son of God. Olympic diving is what I do, but it is not who I am." It is easy to fall into the trap of defining yourself based on performance. Most often, you don't even know you are doing it until that title, role, or achievement is taken away from you.

The first time I realized I was putting my identity in my job was at age twenty-four. I had gone through four years of college to receive my degree in music

---

[2] Henri Nouwen, "Being the Beloved," a sermon given in the early 1990's at the Crystal Cathedral, YouTube video, https://www.youtube.com/watch?v=v8U4V4aaNWk&feature=youtu.be.

education. I landed a job teaching high school choir in a local public high school, but two years into my job I was miserable. I cried every day on my way to school. I faked it really well with my students and their parents, but my husband got the real story.

"If you hate it so much, why don't you quit?" he would ask.

"Because if I do, my whole degree was wasted," I answered.

That was only part of the reason, however. The bigger truth was that I was defined by this job. If I quit, all my colleagues would lose respect for me. What would I tell people at parties when they asked, "What do you do?" I had been offered a church secretary job, but that sounded embarrassing. In my mind, secretary jobs were for people who didn't go to college and get degrees.

Eventually, the job stress won out. I quit teaching and took that church job. It took a while to get over the urge to justify my job transition every time I was asked about it. Many years later, after making this same mistake a few more times, I had to ask myself why I kept answering the "Who am I?" question with "I am what I do." I discovered my tendency to place my identity in my performance comes mainly from the performance-based, legalistic tribe I belonged to growing up.

Knowing where the lie originated was half the battle. The second half was replacing the lie with the truth: I am fully accepted and loved by God, no matter what my career, title, salary, or level of success. Now, I can honestly say no matter what role I am in, I have nothing to prove. *I am not what I do.*

"I am What I Have"

One of our family's favorite books is *A Little Princess* by Frances Hodgson Burnett. The story begins when a little girl, Sara Crewe, whose mother recently died, is sent by her very wealthy father from India to London for schooling. At the school, she is doted on because of her father's wealth, receiving the best room, the honored place at meals, and the admiration of her classmates. Unlike many in her position, though, she was kind to everyone, including her maids and servants. She never flaunted her wealth and she cared for her fellow students by cheering them with fanciful stories.

In one tragic day, she went from princess to servant when she learned of her father's death and loss of every penny. Not only did she give up all her possessions save her treasured doll, she gave up her position of honor at the school and was made to sleep in the cold attic with the servant girl. She went from learning to teaching the younger students, from being served to running errands through the wet dirty London streets wearing an undersized shabby frock.

In her new position, without the trappings of wealth, she was instantly treated like a servant by most of her former classmates. At first, she did not suffer the humiliation well, but she eventually determined that her circumstances would not change her character. "Whatever comes," Sara declared, "cannot alter one thing. If I am a princess in rags and tatters, I can be a princess inside. It would be easy to be a princess if I were dressed in cloth of gold, but it is a great deal more of a triumph to be one all the time when no one knows it."[3]

In all her years as a rich girl, Sara never allowed herself to be defined by her possessions. When those possessions were taken away, she knew the core of her being was the same, no matter how little she owned. How many people waste their best years only to wake up to this reality when they are facing death? How many go to the grave having never learned this? You don't have to be wealthy to fall into this trap of defining yourself by what you have. God warns us about this trap in James 2.

> Suppose a man comes into your meeting wearing a gold ring and fine clothes, and a poor man in filthy old clothes also comes in. If you show special attention to the man wearing fine clothes and say, "Here's a good seat for you," but say to the poor man, "You stand there" or "Sit on the floor by my feet," have you not discriminated among yourselves and become judges with evil thoughts? Listen, my dear brothers and sisters: Has not God chosen those who are poor in the eyes of the world to be rich in faith and to inherit the kingdom he promised those who love him?[4]

Don't wait until you are in heaven standing shoulder to shoulder with every earthly class of Christian to learn *you are not what you have.*

---

[3] Frances Hodgson Burnett, *A Little Princess* (New York: Barnes & Noble, 2012), 138.
[4] James 2:1–5

"I am What People Think of Me"

On August 17, 2014, Rob Limon was shot dead in the railway office where he worked. It didn't take detectives long to put the pieces together: his wife, Sabrina, was discovered to be having an affair with the man who pulled the trigger. As is the case with every murderous love triangle, the question everyone asked was, "Why not just divorce him? Why did you feel you had to kill him?" The surprising answer in this case was she didn't want her small-town friends to think she was a bad person for divorcing her husband. As crazy as it sounds, she reasoned that as long as they didn't get caught for the murder, she could have it all—a new spouse and the respect and love of her friends. Of course, they did get caught and she lost the admiration that she was willing to kill for in order to maintain.

Living for external affirmation and acceptance is a major issue in today's image-obsessed world, but it is not a new problem. What is the solution? Socrates said, "The best way to gain a good reputation is to endeavor to be what you desire to appear." In other words, a good reputation is the by-product of sound character. This is certainly true, but if we focus only on superior morals and a well-disciplined private life, we do not go far enough. I know many non-Christians who have sound character and a good reputation. C.S. Lewis has a chapter in *Mere Christianity* titled "Nice People or New Men" where he addresses the need for Christ to completely transform us, not merely make us nicer versions of ourselves.

Niceness—wholesome, integrated personality—
is an excellent thing. We must try by every med-
ical, educational, economic, and political means
in our power, to produce a world where as many
people as possible grow up "nice"; just as we
must try to produce a world where all have
plenty to eat. But we must not suppose that even
if we succeeded in making everyone nice we
should have saved their souls. A world of nice
people, content in their own niceness, looking no
further, turned away from God, would be just as
desperately in need of salvation as a miserable
world—and might even be more difficult to save.[5]

Just as God doesn't care how many likes we receive on social media or compliments we get from
people we admire, he also doesn't care how many private virtues we practice if we are simply working hard
to be good apart from him. Timothy Keller likes to say
there are two barriers that keep people from the gospel—religion and irreligion. Religion is the more
insidious barrier because our goodness makes us unaware of our need for a Savior.[6] This need becomes
glaringly apparent when we explore motivation. If we
are honest with ourselves, most of our "good deeds"
are motivated by either pride or fear—pride of being
better than others or fear of being punished. If you
are a pretty good person, the sooner you see the selfish motives for your goodness the better off you'll be
because you will understand more clearly your need
for a Savior.

---

[5] C.S. Lewis, *Mere Christianity* (New York: MacMillan
Publishing Company, 1952), 167.
[6] Timothy Keller, *Prodigal God: Recovering the Heart of the
Christian Faith* (New York: Penguin Group, 2008).

If appearing to be good is not enough and trying hard to be good apart from Christ is not enough, what is the solution for the problem of living for external validation? If you are a child of God, you are hidden with Christ, resting in his righteousness. *You are positionally good with God,* having done nothing to earn that favor. You have nothing to prove to him, yourself, or anyone else. Now, not only are you good with God but God is also making you into a new person.

C.S. Lewis said, "God looks at you as if you were a little Christ: Christ stands beside you to turn you into one."[7] When you give yourself fully over to him, he promises to chip away at the rough edges of your soul until one day, in your glorified state, you will look into Christ's eyes and see in them your own reflection.[8] This is what Christ meant when he said, "Whoever wants to save their life will lose it, but whoever loses their life for me and for the gospel will save it."[9] When you lose yourself in him, you will find your true self. With your identity firmly planted in Christ, you will be unconcerned with appearing to be good, and you will be unconcerned with trying to be good. Your only concern will be surrendering to the transforming chisel of the Holy Spirit as he forms you into the little Christ that God already sees you to be.

When we can learn to live this way—aware of our weakness but also aware of our secure position in Christ—we will be able to confidently say: *I am not what people think about me.*

Of course, we don't usually consciously answer the "Who are you?" question with one of these three

---

[7] Lewis, *Mere Christianity*, 151.
[8] 2 Corinthians 3:16–18
[9] Mark 8:34–35

wrong answers. Anyone who has been a Christian for a while knows the "church" answer to that question is "I am a child of God." But do our lives reflect this answer? Or are we living as though our identity is in our performance, possessions, or reputation?

Let's look to an Old Testament prophet for an example of someone who actually lived out his identity as a child of God.

Jeremiah's Two Trees

The life of an Old Testament prophet was lonely and difficult, and Jeremiah's life was no exception. Jeremiah is known as the weeping prophet because he was called to the excruciating task of declaring the famine, plunder, and exile of God's people if they did not repent of their idolatry, greed, and disobedience. Turns out people didn't like Jeremiah or his message very much. The priests conspired to kill him for exposing their sin.[10] God protected him from death by revealing their plans but warned him his persecution would only get worse. Later, he suffered humiliation when another priest had him beaten and put in public stocks for a day.[11] Another time, he was thrown into a cistern in mud up to his neck and left to starve to death, but an Ethiopian slave rescued him.[12] The king imprisoned him to keep him quiet, and he was kept under guard until the Babylonians eventually invaded Jerusalem in 587 BC and captured his people. His Babylonian captors let him go free and showed

---

[10] Jeremiah 11
[11] Jeremiah 20
[12] Jeremiah 26

him more kindness than his own Israelite tribe,[13] which probably made Jeremiah feel even more isolated and lonely.

Imagine the pain Jeremiah must have felt when his national tribe abandoned and persecuted him. That pain probably paled in comparison to having his closest family members betray him.[14] With not even the love of a wife and family to console him (God had forbidden him to marry[15]), he complained to God that the task was too great, the price too high. "Why does the way of the wicked prosper? Why do all the faithless live in ease?"[16] "I have neither lent nor borrowed, yet everyone curses me."[17] "Think of how I suffer reproach for your sake."[18] "Why is my pain unending and my wound grievous and incurable?"[19] "I am ridiculed all day long; everyone mocks me . . . The word of the Lord has brought me insult and reproach all day long."[20] He even went so far as to question his very existence. "Why did I ever come out of the womb to see trouble and sorrow and to end my days in shame?"[21]

It would be natural for Jeremiah to internalize the rejection from his people and the harsh criticism of his peers and form an identity of weakness and shame, but he did not. In times of his greatest suffering, Jeremiah recalled the moment he was called by God. "Before I formed you in the womb, I knew you,"

---

[13] Jeremiah 40:2–4
[14] Jeremiah 12:6
[15] Jeremiah 16:1–2
[16] Jeremiah 12:1
[17] Jeremiah 15:10
[18] Jeremiah 15:15
[19] Jeremiah 15:18
[20] Jeremiah 20:8
[21] Jeremiah 20:18

God had said. "Before you were born I set you apart."[22] Jeremiah understood his identity was not self-declared or bestowed on him by the people around him. It was given to him by God. "I bear your name,"[23] he reminded God in the midst of his complaining. God offered him only one assurance: "I am with you."[24] Not "I will bless you" or even "I will protect you," but "I am with you." God's presence was enough to sustain Jeremiah when he was at his lowest. He could endure any earthly assault as long as he remembered, "A man's life is not his own,"[25] and constantly fell back to his God-given identity.

Drawn from his personal experience with loneliness and suffering, this is Jeremiah's story of two trees:

This is what the Lord says: "Cursed is the one who trusts in man, who draws strength from mere flesh and whose heart turns away from the Lord. That person will be like a bush in the wastelands; they will not see prosperity when it comes. They will dwell in the parched places of the desert, in a salt land where no one lives.

But blessed is the one who trusts in the Lord, whose confidence is in him. They will be like a tree planted by the water that sends out its roots by the stream. It does not fear when heat comes; its leaves are always green. It has no worries in a year of drought and never fails to bear fruit."[26]

---

[22] Jeremiah 1:4–5
[23] Jeremiah 15:15,16
[24] Jeremiah 1:20, 15:20
[25] Jeremiah 10:23
[26] Jeremiah 17:5–8

While the trees are obviously metaphors for two different types of people, I like to think of the roots of the tree as the human search for identity. When we look to "mere flesh" (i.e., ourselves or other people) for identity, we are like the sagebrush: uprooted and tumbling through life, disillusioned, skeptical, insecure, thirsty, and lonely. When the trials of life come, if our search for identity has gone no further than what we do, what we have, or what people think of us, we will wither.

When the roots of our lives have found the spring of God's love and acceptance, we are like the mighty sycamore planted by the stream. We are daily tapping into the source through prayer and contemplation in the Word. When the trials come, and we can be sure they will, rather than being uprooted, we will dig deeper and draw nourishment from our eternal well. Instead of withering, we will stay alive. Instead of toppling, we will sway and even bend, but we will remain rooted. Grounded in the knowledge of who we are, we can live abundant, fruitful, joy-filled, confident, open-hearted lives.

You may read about the sycamore and think, "I don't always feel joyful and confident. I wonder if I'm really rooted in Christ." Remember Jeremiah's story. His sorrow and weakness was immortalized for us to read generations later. He was raw and honest about his pain. And yet, he wrote about the tree whose leaves are always green and never fails to bear fruit. The key, Jeremiah would affirm, is to stay connected to the river. Keep reminding yourself who you are and who God is.

You Have a Choice

I want to leave you with this full assurance: you can decide which tree you want to be. You may have believed lies about your identity—lies stemming from the story of the love you received, the tribes you belonged to, or the voices you listened to—but you can decide whether or not you will continue believing those lies. You are not a victim of your story. You have the power—not in yourself, but in the eternal spring of God—to shed those labels and boldly replace them with the only one that matters: *I am a beloved and accepted child of God.*

Reflection Questions

1. Which of the three identity traps do you tend to fall into most—I am what I do, I am what I have, or I am what others think of me? Is there some part of your story that makes it difficult to avoid that trap?

2. What are some tangible ways you can plant your life beside the Living Water so that you can flourish and remain steady amidst assaults on your God-given identity?

ACKNOWLEDGMENTS

O ur accomplishments are never ours alone. There is always at least one cheerleader, mentor, teacher, or coach behind every finished product. In my case, there was a whole army of them. *Tracing the Thread* is a culmination of a three-year journey, birthed from my year as a C.S. Lewis Institute fellow. Thank you to Steve Anderson for your faithful direction of the Seattle chapter, and to my patient mentor and excellent listener, Sandy Hanson. The core ideas for the book began as a women's day-long teaching intensive at Seed Church in Seattle, then expanded to include gathering stories from willing congregants. Thank you to those who shared your stories with me. I consider them a sacred gift, and can only hope I stewarded them well.

The act of writing a book, though much more time-consuming than I ever imagined, was the most enjoyable part of this process. Thank you to my husband Brent, and our four children, Ian, Sylas, Alex, and Ameris, for giving me the focused time I needed to get my thoughts down on paper, as well as the feedback and encouragement necessary to keep working.

For me, the much more difficult aspect of writing a book was getting it out into the world. Thank you to my first editor, Jay Pearson, not only for your technical expertise, but also for believing this book was important and necessary. Thank you to my author friends for pointing me in the right direction regarding book proposals, agents, conferences, one-sheets, elevator pitches, book launches, and so much more. I simply needed to ask, and a wealth of information was eagerly shared about all things publishing from too many friends to count.

Thank you to Jeremy Writebol from Gospel Centered Discipleship for finding my book online and allowing me the opportunity to eventually hold it in the flesh and share it with a wider audience. Thank you to the incredible editors at GCD for your careful and serious treatment of this project. You have made it a hundred times better.

Lastly, thank you to my parents, Mike and Linda whose unwavering bedrock support began years before I ever thought to write a book, and continues to this day.

ABOUT THE AUTHOR

Christy Rood, her husband Brent, and their two small children moved coast-to-coast in 2002 to plant a church in the Seattle area. Fifteen years, two more children, and many faith-building experiences later, God called them away from their church, back into business, and back across the country to Raleigh, North Carolina.

Christy credits her years as a church planter with teaching her the most valuable lesson of her life – to find her identity, not in people-pleasing, not in the affirmation (or lack thereof) of ministry success, not even in doing good things for the Kingdom of God, but simply in being who she is: a Child of God. The theme of identity has been a major one in her life and ministry, and she finds herself frequently encouraging others with what God had taught her.

You can find Christy's blog at www.christyjrood.com, or connect with her on Twitter (@christyrood), Facebook (@ChristyJRood), or Instagram (@christyjrood).

ABOUT GOSPEL-CENTERED DISCIPLESHIP

You may have noticed that there are a lot of resources available for theological education, church planting, and missional church, but not for discipleship. We noticed too, so we started Gospel-Centered Discipleship to address the need for reliable resources on a whole range of discipleship issues.

When we use the term "gospel-centered," we aren't trying to divide Christians into camps, but to promote a way of following Jesus that is centered on the gospel of grace. While all disciples of Jesus believe the gospel is central to Christianity, we often live as if religious rules or spiritual license actually form the center of discipleship.

Jesus calls us to displace those things and replace them with the gospel. We're meant to apply the benefits of the gospel to our lives every day, not to merely bank on them for a single instance of "being saved." A gospel-centered disciple returns to the gospel over and over again, to receive, apply, and spread God's forgiveness and grace into every aspect of life.

GOSPEL-CENTERED
DISCIPLESHIP RESOURCES

Visit GCDiscipleship.com/Books.

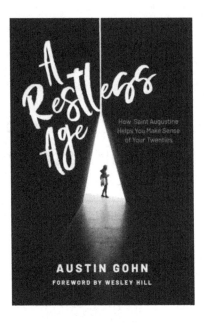

Do your twenties feel restless? You're not the first young adult to feel this way. Saint Augustine describes the same struggle in his Confessions, the most-read spiritual memoir in history. He experimented with different religious options, tried to break destructive habits, struggled to find the right friends, experienced a devastating breakup, and nearly burned out in his career—all before his thirty-second birthday. He spent his twenties looking for rest in all the wrong places.

In *A Restless Age*, Austin Gohn wades through Augustine's *Confessions* to show us how the five searches of young adulthood—answers, habits, belonging, love, and work—are actually searches for rest. "Our heart is restless," Augustine writes, "until it finds rest in you."

Kelly Havrilla

The Christian life is knowing God. It is not an impersonal knowledge of bare facts but one rooted in wonder at "the light of the knowledge of the glory of God in the face of Jesus Christ" (2 Cor. 4:6). It is knowing that basks in the glories of the gospel.

In *Gospel Glories from A to Z*, Kelly Havrilla works to reflect some of that glory onto each page as she connects deep biblical truths through the structure of the alphabet. Useful for both those new to the beauty of Christianity and those looking for a fresh way to grow deeper this book aims to make God's grace abundantly clear and accessible. Our hope is that this reflection will spark a desire to venture into deeper waves of gospel glories.

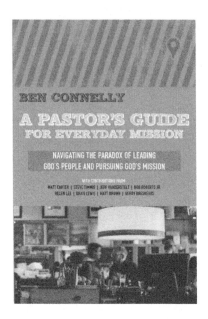

After fifteen plus years of vocational ministry, Ben Connelly had an epiphany. He had missed the great commission. He was really good at keeping Christians happy and really bad at making disciples. *A Pastor's Guide to Everyday Mission* helps those in paid ministry positions rediscover—and live—their life as God's missionaries, even as they minister to God's people.

Too often we limit the power of the gospel to its blessings for us in the afterlife. We fail to see how the power of God, which raised Jesus from the dead, fuels our day-to-day battle against sin in this life. *Renew* shows us the grace of God is able to change us now.

For those looking to break specific sinful habits and temptations as well as those looking to gain a better grasp of how a Christian grows, *Renew* speaks to the power of the gospel today.

Made in the USA
Columbia, SC
06 May 2020

94547424R00117